THE GREEN LINE

THE GREEN
LINE

VIEWS FROM SPORT'S MOST OUTSPOKEN COMMENTATOR

Alan Green

HEADLINE

First published in 2000
by HEADLINE BOOK PUBLISHING

10 9 8 7 6 5 4 3 2 1

British Library Cataloguing in Publication Data

Green, Alan
The green line: views from sport's most outspoken
commentator
1. Green, Alan 2. Sports – Miscellaneous
I. Title
796

ISBN 0 7472 1618 5

Typeset by Avon Dataset Ltd, Bidford-on-Avon, Warks

Printed and bound in Great Britain by
Mackays of Chatham plc, Chatham, Kent

HEADLINE BOOK PUBLISHING
A division of Hodder Headline
338 Euston Road
London NW1 3BH

www.headline.co.uk
www.hodderheadline.com

CONTENTS

CHAPTER ONE

BEGINNINGS

E very now and then I have to pinch myself to appreciate how fortunate I am to be a sports commentator. Looking around the fantastic Stade de France on the night of the 1998 World Cup final, there was a temptation to believe it was all a dream, that I'd soon wake up to find myself back in Belfast, in more humble circumstances, earning a living as a teacher or a chemist or whatever. It's a feeling that comes to my mind more often than you'd believe.

Yet, more than the glamorous venues, the great sporting occasions, what makes me truly thankful is what I read in the letters that I receive from young people.

Dear Alan,
The thing I want most in life is your job. Please tell me what I must do to become a football commentator.
Yours sincerely . . .

That's when the guilt sets in. You see, I never actually wanted to be a football commentator. How can I explain that it just happened? That none of it was planned, certainly not by me?

★ ★ ★

When I was a boy, growing up in Northern Ireland, my career fantasy was about being a pilot. That, I thought, would bring me all the glamour and the travel that I craved. It was a desire that stayed with me until I became a diabetic at the age of twelve, dismissing any remote prospect I had of flying an aeroplane.

It's true that I loved sport, all sport. When I wasn't out watching Linfield in the Irish League, I'd be in the living-room glued to *Grandstand* or *Sportsnight* on the television, or carrying a transistor radio around the house listening to *Sports Report* or whatever game was on that night. My early teens were swamped with the sounds of Raymond Glendenning and Maurice Edleston but I never, ever thought of being one of them. That was for others, not for a Belfast schoolboy with a harsh Ulster accent.

I don't honestly remember what sparked my interest in journalism. Perhaps it was the habit my father had of slowing down the car each time we passed the offices of the *Belfast Telegraph*, catching the latest news headlines on a succession of billboards. I tried to imagine what was going on behind those big windows – reporters dealing with world news stories as well as local ones – and how no two days would be the same. Variety equals excitement. Now, *that* could be for me.

When I was fifteen, I wrote to the *Telegraph* asking for a summer job when term broke up at Methodist College. I had no contacts at the newspaper and I didn't even have a decent reason for asking. I can barely remember the interview I was given but I do vividly recall how excited I felt walking in that first morning in July 1967, seeing that huge open-plan newsroom and the reporters banging away at their typewriters.

I was paid very little, barely enough for pocket-money, and my work as a copy-boy could hardly be described as significant. I collected the stories from the reporters, once they'd been written up, and either passed them on to a different desk to be sub-edited or folded them neatly into a container which disappeared down a chute. I never found out where the other end was. I assumed it was at the printing end of the building.

It was wonderful; I found it such a privilege knowing what the news was before my parents and friends could read about it. Each day, I learnt something new about the business, even if it was only how to snap the cap off a beer bottle using the corner of a filing cabinet! It never struck me how stupid it was not to have a bottle-opener in the office. How could I question anything? Here I was, working in the company of worldly wise, hard-nosed journalists. This was the life for me.

Partly because I had developed something of an encyclopaedic knowledge of local sport, I was soon adopted by the sports desk and, in particular, by the then sports editor, Malcolm Brodie. What started as a friendship between master and pupil has now lasted over thirty years. I owe Malcolm a huge amount for the support and advice he's given me throughout my career. He is an incredible man and a very great journalist who's covered every World Cup since 1954. There aren't too many still around who've done that.

The stories about him are legendary. For me, two stand out. Both arose during a trip to South America with England in the late fifties. Communications then were the bane of a reporter's life, with no lap-top computers or mobile phones. Watching an event and deciding what you would write or say about it was the easiest part of the job. Getting in touch with the office was the really difficult bit. Brodie had spent hours trying to get through to the *Telegraph* on a dodgy telephone line. Eventually, the switchboard answered: 'Hallo, *Belfast Telegraph* . . .'

'Malcolm Brodie,' he replied.

'Sorry,' the operator said, 'he's in South America,' and cut the connection!

When he finally got through again, this time he reached the copy-taker. Brodie, waxing lyrical about the performance of a young player called Pelé, began: 'Magnifico! Magnifico! Magnifico!'

'It's all right, Malcolm,' chipped in the copy-taker, 'I heard you the first time!'

Brodie took me under his wing. Aside from the summer job, which happened every year after that, I started to write occasional match reports for the paper at weekends, mostly hockey – the game I played at school – and cricket. By the time I'd left Methodist College and taken my degree in Modern History at Queen's University, Belfast, there wasn't the slightest doubt about how I wanted to earn my living. I wanted to be a reporter for the *Belfast Telegraph*, though not in sport, however much I enjoyed that; instead in news.

I applied to be taken on as a Thomson trainee. The Thomson Group had newspapers throughout Britain, but I was set on the one job which I knew was up for grabs at the *Telegraph* and I was reasonably confident of getting it. Nevertheless, like all graduates, I adopted the machine-gun approach to job applications: fire off as many as you can in the hope that you'll hit more than one target.

So I might have ended up as a departmental manager with Marks and Spencer. Actually, I got to the final interview, where the chief interrogator asked me which area I wished to specialise in. That was a difficult one, since I wasn't all that interested in the job. I told him 'market research', whereupon he told me that Marks and Spencer didn't do any. You could have picked me up off the floor. How could they know what their customers liked and disliked if they didn't try to find out? I wasn't surprised that I didn't get the job.

I went closer with the Inland Revenue. I know, you can just imagine me as a tax inspector! Yet, again, I reached the final stage, and though I was never going to accept the position, I was genuinely surprised that I didn't get the offer. Months afterwards, I bumped into one of the people who'd interviewed me. He asked me what I was doing and I told him that I was about to move to London to work for the BBC. Smiling, he said: 'Oh, we got it right after all, then.'

'What do you mean?' I asked.

'We'd have given you the job but we sensed that your real interests lay elsewhere. After you left the room, we agreed that you probably wanted to be a journalist.' He was right, of course, but he couldn't have imagined what I'd gone through.

I hadn't remotely considered the BBC as an option. It was the university careers officer who suggested I apply. Now that, I thought, would be a waste of time. Everyone knew it was horrendously difficult to get accepted for their news training scheme. Thousands applied and the BBC took on, at that time, only sixteen graduates a year. I didn't think I was nearly good enough, but I stuck the form in the post anyway. It wouldn't matter, I was going to get the *Telegraph* job, I thought. I didn't; I came second. It was an awful blow. It felt like the end of my world. Any confidence I had in myself was shattered and I couldn't think what I would do next.

Out of the blue, I received a letter from the BBC asking me to attend a medical in London. I couldn't think why. I'd been to a couple of interviews, in Belfast and at Broadcasting House in London, but there seemed no reason to believe they were seriously interested in me. This, however, was unusual. Why did they think it worthwhile spending the money to fly me to London just to see a doctor who'd check out my diabetes?

Naturally, I went and, to my huge surprise, the BBC offered me a job. I still wasn't sure, particularly about my ability, so I rang Malcolm Brodie. He thought that I'd have walked the *Telegraph* position and was disappointed that I hadn't. Malcolm offered me a job as a sub-editor on his sports desk at a salary nearly twice what the BBC was offering. By now, my head was spinning. I asked him for time to think about it.

I did a lot of thinking. The *Telegraph* would be giving me more money and I knew I could do the job there. It was safe; it was 'home'. But the BBC? London? It was a city that I didn't know, overwhelming in size and complexity to a boy like me from the sticks. I'd be lost, unsure of where I was and where I was going. So don't ask me why I chose the BBC!

My first day of work at Broadcasting House, on 1 April 1975, almost persuaded me that I'd made a huge mistake. I was surrounded by people on the course who seemed so much more capable than me. Joshua Rosenberg, until recently the BBC's legal affairs correspondent, was already a fully qualified lawyer. His wife, Melanie Phillips, a brilliant columnist with the *Sunday Times*, had been turned down by the BBC for the same course. David Powers, who became the Tokyo correspondent, spoke fluent Russian and Japanese. With my broad accent, they could hardly make out what I was saying in English. In those first few months, I tried desperately to hang on to their coat-tails. I felt inadequate, unfit to work alongside these people, but every journalist will tell you a story of how they got their break. I needed one and, thankfully, it came along.

There were eight people in my group and every day we would put together a dummy version of *The World At One* or *PM*. We'd take turns at being editor, producer, reporter and so on. This day, I was the reporter. When I got into the office, there was news of a rail crash near Clapham and I was assigned to the story.

News trainees weren't, in those days, particularly well liked by the regular journalists within the BBC. We were seen as spoilt brats, always being spoon-fed, never having had to learn the trade as they had had to do, moving up through the ranks of local newspapers before making it on the national stage. I remember once, when I was moaning about the difficulty in surviving on the pittance of my BBC salary, being berated by Michael Cole, a particularly pompous prat who seemed well suited to his future role as royal correspondent and then spokesman for Mohammed Al-Fayed. 'You're privileged,' he said to me, 'you should work for the BBC for nothing.'

Most of the more reasonable journalists had a point, most news trainees had never worked on newspapers, but this was precisely why the BBC set up its scheme. It didn't want its future journalists to be writers turned broadcasters. It wanted 'virgins', unsullied by newspaper clichés, who they could mould into proper broadcast journalists, and the notion that we were given the best of everything was nonsense. Typically, news trainees, making dummy programmes, weren't allowed to use taxis. We were supposed to cover stories taking a bus or a train. It certainly saved money, but it was also ridiculously impractical. How the hell was I expected to get to Clapham quickly without using a cab? I couldn't. So I took one anyway and decided that I'd argue about it later.

I got to Clapham before anybody else. It wasn't a serious incident, but I was able to establish the facts and do some interviews before the other reporters arrived. In the circumstances, I was feeling pretty pleased with myself, until I realised there was no easy way back to Broadcasting House. There wasn't a taxi to be seen. There wasn't even a bus to jump on. Suddenly, I saw a BBC radio car arriving. Basically, these were black taxis which had been refurbished as mobile studios, ideal for a job like this where news had to be fed back as quickly as possible.

Out jumped the reporter, Geoffrey Wareham. Could I, grovelling, hitch a lift back to BH? 'Of course, dear boy,' was the reply, 'as soon as I've done my work.' As he was about to go to precisely where the train had crashed, the phone rang in the radio car. It was the producer of the Jimmy Young programme on Radio 2. Would Geoffrey do a live report into the show in about thirty seconds' time. 'No,' said Geoffrey, 'but I know someone who can.' I didn't have time to think. If I had, I'd probably have run away. Instead, I lifted the microphone and spoke to Jimmy Young, live and on national radio. I was sweating profusely. I remember getting a mild electric shock when the lip microphone touched my face but I don't recall what I said. I'm sure it wasn't very good. It didn't matter to me.

I returned to the office, a hero to my colleagues. To that date, none of them had had such exposure and they were all very envious. In their eyes, I'd made it. Indeed, it was a turning point for me. I never, ever felt inadequate again. I started to enjoy broadcasting instead of being frightened by it. I started to relax and became confident to be me.

I did various attachments around the BBC, local radio, regional television, national newsrooms, to help me decide which area I wanted to work in permanently. The BBC was also deciding, more relevantly, which area they wanted me to work in. Thankfully, our interests coincided. I fancied writing for television news and they thought I'd be suitable. I was told I'd be given the first available vacancy as a scriptwriter, a humble enough beginning to my ambition of becoming editor of the *Nine O'Clock News*.

In the meantime, I was asked to go to Belfast to work on the local television programme, *Scene Around Six*. They wanted someone to establish, produce and present a nightly sports desk. Me. I was interested, but only as a temporary diversion. Yet it went better than they or I expected and, within a few weeks, my face was well known on local television. I don't think it went to my head – I certainly had no ideas that I should work in sport – but it did change my thinking, not least because I preferred Belfast to London.

When I was asked to become the main presenter of radio current affairs in Northern Ireland, I didn't hesitate to say yes. The province was in the midst of the Troubles and I would be certain to learn a lot about broadcasting, very quickly. This was an area, after all, where other news trainees such as Jeremy Paxman, Nicholas Witchell and James Robbins had cut their teeth.

I loved the work but not the hours. Getting up at four o'clock every morning to present *Good Morning Ulster* wreaked havoc with my body and I lasted just ten months before gratefully moving into the newsroom as a television reporter. I was back on course for my *Nine O'Clock News* ambition.

People outside the province must imagine that the late seventies would have been a traumatic time to be living in Ulster. The IRA campaign was at its height, with a daily ritual of killings and bombings. Strangely, most of us, even reporters, lived a fairly normal existence. Of course, life was constantly disrupted by road blocks and bomb scares but people learnt to adjust and take such matters into account planning their daily routines. I lived in Bangor, a lovely seaside town a dozen miles from Belfast, and largely it was untouched by the Troubles. It may seem amazing but not once in the thirty happy years I lived in Northern Ireland before moving to England, did I see a bomb go off 'live', not even as a reporter.

I have vivid memories of my time in the Belfast newsroom, some mixing tragedy with typical Ulster wit. One afternoon, just before four o'clock, I was dispatched with a film crew to Newry, about forty miles away, where a soldier in the Ulster Defence Regiment had been murdered. By the time we got there, the scene of the incident had been cordoned off and, apart from bloodstains on the road, little evidence of the crime remained. My job, as a reporter, was to ensure that general pictures were taken of the area as well as doing a 'piece-to-camera', me looking at the camera saying what had happened.

We were drastically short of time. The programme began at 5.55 p.m., immediately after the national news on BBC 1. We arrived back at Broadcasting House only twenty minutes before transmission. The film – there was little videotape then – was developed rapidly and rushed into the cutting room, where a few scenes were edited together including my piece-to-camera. I was to supply a voice-over for the general pictures and hurriedly scribbled the relevant words. As usual, the lift was occupied elsewhere, so I had to run up the four flights of stairs to get to the studio. This was to be the lead item. I was out of breath when I grabbed a chair beside the presenter, Barry Cowan, as the opening titles to the programme were run.

It didn't seem to matter that my shirt and tie were undone and that I had no jacket on, never mind make-up. I was to be 'out-of-vision'. I heard Barry's introduction, '. . . as Alan Green reports,' and looked at the monitor for the pictures. They weren't there! Suddenly, I saw this studio camera, with its tell-tale red light on, moving towards me. Hell, they're coming to me in-vision. Desperately, I tried to button my shirt collar and tighten my tie with one hand while holding the script in the other. I had to give up. There I was, talking about a murder in a disgracefully dishevelled state. I never forgave the director. He could have gone to any other item and saved my report till later.

Fully a fortnight after that, I answered the door to my flat in Bangor to a man who'd come to read the electricity meter. 'Don't I know you?' he said. 'You're on television, aren't you?' I nodded. '*Scene Around Six*, isn't it? You're the guy who talked about that murder with your tie undone!' Only in Northern Ireland could you laugh about such matters.

Throughout this spell, I continued to do some work for Sport. I would present the local results sequence at the end of *Grandstand* each Saturday. It paid some extra money and, besides, I enjoyed doing it. I didn't really have positive thoughts about switching to

Sport but, for various reasons, I was becoming unsettled in the newsroom. Personal relationships were frequently determining who did which story, ability hardly came into it. The regular news editor, Robin Walsh, was on attachment to London and, on a rare visit back to Belfast, he confronted me when he heard I'd applied for a job in Sport. As we argued about it he even used the word 'traitor'. Perhaps it was as well that my application was successful!

This was 1979, the first of three years working for BBC Northern Ireland Sport. Mostly, it was great fun. I got on really well with the senior radio producer, Brian Dempster, and with Rupert Millar, who produced the television programme that I was co-presenter of and reporter for, *Sportsweek*. The relationship with Joy Williams, Head of Sport, was more strained. I felt she preferred being boss of people who owed her something, and I didn't. The BBC had taken me on long before I met her, so if I thought she was wrong, I said so. She was still in charge and ultimately I did as I was told, but Williams must have had a nagging feeling that I didn't respect her. She was right. Frequently, she gave me a hard time. I remember once asking her if she could get me some tickets (to buy) for the Irish Open golf at Portmarnock, an event to which she made an annual pilgrimage. For many at the BBC it was often seen as an excuse for a booze-up, but I was actually interested in the golf. She refused, offering a stinging rejoinder, 'Darling, you don't think you're ever going to work in golf, do you?' Little did either of us know that one day I would be commentating at the Ryder Cup and the Open Championship.

She did, though, make one crucial decision that affected my career. The regular television football commentator, George Hamilton, was leaving and Williams needed a replacement quickly with the Irish Cup final between Cliftonville and Portadown coming up. 'Would you do it?' she asked.

'No, not a chance,' I replied. 'I may be a presenter and a reporter but I'll *never* be a commentator.'

However, I recognised the problem created by George's departure and agreed to fill in. I thought I was pretty poor, but Williams must have recognised something. On her insistence, I persisted with television commentary. It wasn't exactly an onerous task in Belfast. There were probably only half a dozen opportunities a season. It was pleasant but, I thought, hardly leading to anywhere of significance. Little did I know.

By the end of 1981, I was getting itchy feet. Save for the conflicts with my head of department, I was enjoying my work. The trouble was, I had stopped learning. I knew I had to move on, in reality, had to move away. Though I didn't enjoy London when I had to live there, it was certainly the centre of British broadcasting. I saw jobs advertised for BBC Radio Sport and applied.

To emphasise that my ego wasn't as big as some people seemed to think, I was actually more interested in the producer vacancy than in the broadcasting positions. I believed I was being interviewed for both when I attended the interview in London and wasn't aware that the producer vacancy had already been filled.

'Slim' Wilkinson was Head of Radio Sport, an engaging man who'd made his reputation as the television producer at Wimbledon. I'm not sure exactly how much he knew about radio, but he was easy to work for. He rang me to say that, unfortunately, he couldn't offer me a job in London, as the positions had already been earmarked for Mike Ingham, Ian Darke and Tony Adamson. Would I, though, consider working in Manchester as Radio Sport's 'man in the north of England'? My immediate response was to say thanks but no. If I was going to have to move to London, new wife Brenda in tow, it would be much better to make it in one hop, not two, and I could only consider Manchester to be an intermediate step. He asked me to think it over and, in the meantime, to fly to England to talk to the future Controller of Radio 4, Michael Green, who was then Head of Network Radio in Manchester. Michael was wonderfully persuasive and I was hooked.

The job title, and certainly the responsibilities, have changed more than once but, for eighteen years, in Macclesfield if not in Manchester, there I have remained. The variety of my time in network radio will unfold in the pages to come but, at the outset, one vital factor must be explained: I did not want to be a radio commentator. I started working in Manchester on 1 February 1982, and I was astounded to hear that I was expected to commentate for Radio 2 on England versus Northern Ireland at Wembley on 23 February. This wasn't part of the deal. I thought I was to be a reporter and feature maker, but I wasn't given a choice. My name was on the rota for the game and that was that.

If I thought my first television commentary was ordinary, it was outstanding compared to my opening efforts on radio. I couldn't get my head around the lack of pictures. Why should I tell you that there's a free-kick when you can see it for yourself? This wasn't clever radio commentary. Worse, Bryan Robson scored for England in the opening minutes and I barely recognised him. I stumbled through the game, overwhelmed by the brilliance of the main commentator, Peter Jones, who sat alongside me.

I remember going back to my hotel near Piccadilly Circus with Brian Dempster, who was in London for the game. We drank far too much gin that night. I was seriously depressed, though Brian assured me I would definitely become a good radio commentator. I couldn't agree. Indeed, I didn't want to pick up a lip microphone ever again.

Someone must know, though I don't, who decided that I should continue commentating. I owe them such a lot. Gradually, as with television, the pain of my performances eased. Commentary became something I looked forward to. I was still concentrating on the basics, who's playing, where's the ball, what's the score, and any injection of my own personality was minimal, but I suppose I was doing an increasingly competent job.

In the early to mid-eighties, Mike Ingham and I were the 'second rank' behind Peter and the football correspondent, Bryon Butler. There were two landmarks signifying my advancement and change of status. Around 1984, I was at Tottenham Hotspur with Bryon for a second-half commentary on *Sport on 2*. Rob Bonnet, who's made a very successful career in television since then, was the football producer. Quietly, he took me to one side. 'You're to finish the game, Alan.' This is always considered the senior role in radio, the better commentator seen as the person best suited to describe the climax to a game. So when we are working together, Mike Ingham and I alternate finishing, but when we are working with other commentators we would finish. To this day, I don't know how this particular change was explained to Bryon. He never said.

Peter Jones, though, continued to be the master. Peter had a wonderful command of the English language. He painted beautiful 'pictures' for the listener, even if some of them weren't literally true. One day at Hillsborough, he talked of this dapper gentleman sitting three rows in front of us, wearing a tall blue and white striped top hat. I searched in vain for this gentleman. He wasn't there. It's not a technique that I would employ – real life provides equally good material. You don't need to make it up, though, in fairness, Peter's tales didn't do anyone any harm. He always told the truth when it mattered and no one has ever enthralled the football audience the way he did.

I was at Molineux on the Saturday afternoon of 1 April 1990 to commentate on Wolves against Leeds. Peter was at the Boat Race. I was concentrating on the game, so I was only mildly disturbed at the absence of his voice. When I did realise that I hadn't heard him when I should have done, I called the studio. I was told that Peter had collapsed on the tow-path and that no one knew what condition he was in. He died in the early hours of Sunday morning having suffered a massive stroke.

That day, I was telephoned by Mike Lewis, Head of Radio Sport. Mike was especially close to Peter and was very badly upset. He told me that work had to carry on and things were going to change for me with Peter's death. I was expecting to go to Sheffield in a few days to cover the World Snooker Championship, as I had done every year since 1982. Mike said he was sorry but I was needed on football full time and would have to miss the Crucible. From that day, football commentary became the centre of my working life.

I received a letter many years later from a thirteen-year-old boy, Sam Stevens. He was a bit of a fan and asked lots of questions about me and about football commentary. He didn't know quite how relevant his final query was and what poignant memories it provoked: 'When are you going to end?'

CHAPTER TWO

FERGIE
AND ME

You may not believe me, but there isn't a shred of bias in anything I have ever said or written about Manchester United either for or against, and this is a fact that runs contrary to the countless letters of accusation that I receive. However, for at least a decade, Alex Ferguson has given me cause to be prejudiced against the club. I've resisted that temptation, but it should surprise nobody to hear that I intensely dislike Ferguson, and I wouldn't be surprised if the feeling was mutual. For me, it's become almost a badge of honour.

The relationship wasn't always so sour. When I was taking my first serious steps into football commentary, I was dispatched to Aberdeen to record progress in their victorious European Cup-Winners' Cup campaign in 1982–83. Alongside producer Peter Lorenzo and summariser Frank McLintock, the former Arsenal and Scotland captain, I spent some memorable nights at Pittodrie describing victories for the Scottish Cup holders against the likes of Bayern Munich. They were evenings that stumbled into mornings in the company of the then Aberdeen manager, Alex Ferguson, and his assistant, Archie Knox.

Because Frank and Peter both knew Alex well, we were invited to join in the private after-match celebrations at hotels where licensing hours were conveniently forgotten. I didn't like vodka but I learnt to drink it in Alex's presence, in copious amounts. Alex was great company, witty, at times charming, and certainly fascinating because of his love for, and knowledge of, football. It was a very bright, though misleading, beginning to an association that has figured hugely in my commentary career.

Ferguson was appointed manager at Manchester United in November 1986 in succession to Ron Atkinson. Ron produced attractive sides that won the FA Cup in 1983 and 1985, but the League Championship eluded him as it had done every United boss since 1967. The old First Division of the 1980s was dominated by the 'Merseyside mafia' of Everton and Liverpool and the Old Trafford chairman, Martin Edwards, saw Alex as the man who could break their monopoly. After all, Ferguson had managed a similar feat in Scotland, where he had wrested control from the Glasgow 'old firm' of Celtic and Rangers. Why could he not do the same in England?

I remember vividly his arrival at United. Old Trafford wasn't then quite as spectacular an arena as it has since become, but it was still awe-inspiring, even for someone who had played in front of capacity crowds at Ibrox. After the press conference, I walked down the players' tunnel with Alex on to the pitch where he posed for photographers. The floodlights were on because of the dull wintry afternoon sky. He looked up and around, appearing somewhat overwhelmed by what he saw. 'Do you know,' I asked, 'the size of what you've taken on?' He smiled and gently nodded his head. It was a huge task but he was aware of it.

As, indeed, he was aware of the need to have friends in the media in those early days. The Manchester press corps, with such an enormous club on its patch, was scarcely less important than the grouping of 'number ones' who were based mainly in London. These northern guys could make or break a manager with their coverage and Ferguson knew few of them. Initially, he was very wary of how he'd be treated. This wasn't a small and easily controlled region such as Aberdeen and he didn't like it. The new manager was suspicious of the faces that appeared daily at United's training headquarters, the Cliff. However, he did know Alan Green.

It was then very important for me to get on with any boss of Manchester United. Not long after I'd moved to England, I had an early spat with Ron Atkinson. It came during the World Cup in Spain in 1982, where I was commentating and he was working for ITV. Late one night, in the Sidi Soler hotel in Valencia, where the Northern Ireland squad was based, I was the subject of merciless teasing. I can't even remember what it was about, but Atkinson, a renowned provocateur and joker, was at the heart of it. Wrongly, I reacted and the affair over-heated, with Ron trying to grab me around the throat. Too much wine had been consumed by all of us.

I hardly slept that night, aware that I'd had serious words with the manager of the biggest club in the country – and barely five months into a new job. Yet I needn't have worried. The following morning, Ron laughed it all off. We acknowledged that we were both at fault. I'd learnt that you could have a right old barney with Atkinson, but that it would be quickly forgotten. Sadly, I soon discovered that this was not the case with his successor. I was astonished a few months ago when Alex, in the aftermath of a row with David Beckham, was quoted as saying that he never holds grudges. This has not been my own experience. Some of those who have had a falling-out with him, such as Neil Webb, Jim Leighton, Paul Ince and Brian Kidd, have been on the receiving end of further harsh comment after they have left United.

Anyway, at first, relations could hardly have been better between Alex and me. I recognised his need for a settling-in period and was generally charitable about developments at Old Trafford. Even when I squirmed at some of his purchases (when people rightly praise Ferguson for buying players like Peter Schmeichel they tend to forget that he also bought Ralph Milne!), I was of a mind to give him the benefit of the doubt. I had no supporter's or reporter's axe to grind. I believed strongly that a healthy Manchester United was important to English football (and still do), particularly during its exclusion from European competition through the dark days that followed the Heysel tragedy.

Scottish clubs still played in Europe and Alex kept an interest in their progress – Aberdeen, of course, but particularly Rangers, the club that I always believed was his true love. Their games were televised, though usually only as highlights in England. So, when the opportunity arose, I would invite Alex, and Archie Knox, whom he'd brought along as his assistant to Old Trafford, to New Broadcasting House on Oxford Road in Manchester. The signal being transmitted to London had to pass through and we could watch the games live and in full over a sandwich and a glass of wine. It gave me a chance to socialise with them both and cement any burgeoning friendship. Alex was always very grateful, though he didn't need to be. I was more than happy to help out.

All the while, Alex was making unsteady progress at United. The supporters seemed unsure of the manager, perhaps unaware of the vital work that was proceeding behind the scenes where a new youth development programme was being set in place. The emergence of Beckham, Giggs, the Nevilles, Scholes and all the other dramatically talented United youngsters, was for the future. The fans wanted success now.

It wasn't happening, and as the supporters became more restless and the media more critical, Ferguson became more sensitive to anything he construed as being unhelpful. But people like myself wouldn't have been doing our jobs properly if we didn't point out where we thought things might be going wrong. Whatever was happening behind the scenes, superficially this manager wasn't delivering. I remain convinced that, had United fallen at any step on the road to the 1990 FA Cup final, Ferguson wouldn't have survived, no matter the massive support offered to him then by Martin Edwards. But United didn't fall, and they beat Crystal Palace in the replay.

That result marked the beginning of a period of unprecedented success, elevating Ferguson to a pedestal where he justifiably bears comparison to Sir Matt Busby. Some put him even higher than that, holding him as the greatest manager of all time. I wouldn't go that far because it is so difficult to compare achievements in different eras and to relate results to circumstances. However, in the run-up to the phenomenal treble of 1999, I was among the early few, if not the first, to argue that Ferguson should be honoured with a knighthood. I must add that I argued the case based only on his contribution to football. I can't think of anyone in the game that I disliked more throughout the nineties and I can trace the feeling back to that win over Palace which, I believe, signalled a turning point in Ferguson's relationship with the media generally and with me in particular. Confidence came with his success and his tone seemed to become more aggressive and arrogant.

The first proper inkling I had that something was amiss came on a freezing cold January evening at the Dell. Manchester United, as holders, had drawn 0–0 with Southampton in a televised FA Cup game played on a bone-hard pitch. I had been commentating and rushed down to the dressing-room area to ask Ferguson for a post-match interview. I waited as he performed for television, the biting cold gnawing at my bones. I felt confident that he'd be in a good mood. After all, his team had played well in the circumstances and, more to the point, I was offering him a nice warm laundry-room in which to conduct the interview.

'Could I have a few minutes for Radio 2, Alex?'

He swore at me and told me, 'You don't pick my team, you bastard!'

I had no idea what had provoked such a response. I knew only that, whatever happened, I was going to stand my ground. I honestly thought he might hit me as the tirade continued. I remember thinking, seeing that a policeman was watching on just a few yards away, if Ferguson did strike me, then I'd make sure he spent the rest of the night in a Southampton police cell.

However, having staged his verbal assault, he moved away. For a minute, I stood stunned. I heard someone call me from over my shoulder and turned to see Neil Webb, the then Manchester United and England midfielder, looking down from the top of the staircase. He'd witnessed the whole scene. 'What's going on?' I said. 'Don't worry about him,' Neil replied.

The player was to have painful run-ins of his own with the manager, decisively over whether he could play in an England international in 1992. That was one of the reasons that led to Webb's subsequent exit from Old Trafford. For now, though, I was more concerned at my own relationship with Ferguson. What had I done?

Well, it took some while to establish the exact cause of the manager's ire. It seems that he hadn't appreciated what I'd said at a previous game involving Manchester United.

Jimmy Armfield, who was still working at the time for the *Daily Express* as well as match summarising for the BBC, had gone to

United's training ground on the Friday for a pre-arranged newspaper interview with Mark Hughes. He had sat in on Ferguson's press conference, listening as the manager told how Hughes wouldn't be fit for the following afternoon but that, contrary to expectation, Steve Bruce would play. Jimmy saw Hughes afterwards and suggested, in the circumstances, that they should postpone their chat. 'What are you talking about?' said Hughes. 'I am playing.'

Jim relayed this story to me and, sure enough, in contradiction of what Ferguson had told the press the previous day, Hughes played and Bruce didn't. Now, perhaps circumstances regarding their respective injuries did alter radically overnight. Perhaps Ferguson wasn't playing silly games and wasn't attempting to mislead the opposition. I didn't know for certain. What I said, in giving out the team news, was that I didn't pay attention any more to news emanating from Old Trafford about United's line-ups, but preferred to see for myself who actually ran out on to the pitch. Ferguson wouldn't have liked that. It was the truth but it didn't reflect well on him. Tough. I don't mind if a manager says nothing – that's his prerogative. Giving out wrong information is something else, and too many managers try to use the press in this way, and I object to it, whoever it is.

Relations seemed to deteriorate rapidly thereafter, though, on reflection, there had been persistent signs before that of an imminent breakdown. To begin with, he has always had a suspicion that I am a Liverpool fan. This came to my attention one telling afternoon at Anfield. United played for most of the second half with only ten men after Colin Gibson was sent off, yet they pulled back from two goals down to draw the match 3–3. Afterwards, I approached Alex to do an interview for *Sports Report*. Plainly, his team's comeback, much against the odds, was the story we wanted to hear.

I made my first attempt to speak to him in the corridor that runs underneath the main stand from the dressing-room area to the players' lounge. Ferguson hurried past me. I didn't know why, but thought I'd give him a few moments and approach him again a little later on. Time was still on my side. It wasn't quite five o'clock. I also needed to talk to Kenny Dalglish on another matter and was chatting to the Liverpool boss when we heard Ferguson speaking nearby to a local radio reporter about 'choking on his vomit as he left Anfield'. This was how he emphasised his belief that referees gave visiting sides nothing at Liverpool. Neither Kenny nor I could ignore what was unfolding.

Dalglish exchanged words with Ferguson as he passed him on the way to his office and then emerged, holding his young daughter in his arms, to suggest to reporters that they would get more sense talking to her than to Alex Ferguson. The fuse was lit. Ferguson was now an interview that I *had* to get.

I followed the United boss up to the directors' guest lounge and asked to see him. He came out. 'What's wrong?' I inquired. 'Has *Sports Report* upset you in any way?'

'No,' he said, 'it's you. I'm not talking to you. You're a Liverpool fan. You are just like all the rest!' Alex can come across as paranoid, even fostering it to build the team spirit that helps United, and subsequent success hasn't diminished the trait. The whole phenomenon of ABUs (Anyone But United) enables him to foster this feeling of United against the world.

At this, Norman Wynn and Richard Bott, experienced old hands at the *News of the World* and the *Sunday Express*, both burst out laughing. I was tempted to as well. Instead, I said, 'Well, if it's me, don't hold that against *Sports Report*. Someone else will do the interview.' Ferguson agreed and came down to the broadcast point.

There were a few minutes to go before he was due to go live so I stood in front of him, looked into his eyes, and told him that I didn't know what he was talking about, emphasising that I didn't understand why he wouldn't talk to me, but he felt he hadn't refused to speak to me at all. So, snatching the microphone away from Peter Slater, the outside-broadcast producer who was always ultra keen to get 'on the air', I conducted the interview. Ferguson was outspoken about his feelings but was perfectly pleasant to me. To this day, I suspect he only did the interview because he'd decided that he had to get this particular message across. Personally, I believe he made up his mind to say what he did before the game was even played and whatever its outcome. Long experience suggests to me that sometimes Alex plans the timing of his outbursts and more outspoken statements. His comments about Leeds United in April 1996 were one such example, designed to ensure that the Yorkshire side didn't let up against United's title rivals Newcastle.

It seems ridiculous, working in the same industry, but Alex and I haven't spoken to one another properly since 1992. The only, very brief, exception was in Turin in 1999 after United had so magnificently won the European Cup semi-final second leg against Juventus. There is a little road bridge outside the Stadio Delle Alpi that runs from the ground to where the official coaches are parked. It is isolated from the public and I was walking along it about ninety minutes after the match had finished. I suddenly realised I was heading straight for Ferguson, who was standing on his own talking animatedly into a mobile phone. Who could blame him? It had been a phenomenal performance. He wanted to tell the world about it. Despite my non-relationship with him, I thought it would be churlish in the extreme not to offer congratulations. I reached to shake his hand: 'Fantastic, Alex. You deserve it. Well done.' He thanked me. I swear he couldn't have known who he was in front of! He was that far gone. So, 1999 doesn't really count.

No, 1992 was the last time I made any proper verbal attempt to retrieve the relationship. Previously, I had written to him explaining that the only club I'd ever felt an affinity towards was Linfield in the Irish League. I pointed out that they provoked no personal bias whatsoever when it came to doing my job in England. He actually rang my home to say everything would be okay. But the truce did not last.

Most of the time, we merely avoided each other. It was certainly by accident that I met him at a Danish press conference during the European Championship in Sweden that year. Typically, for there are few more dedicated to his profession, Ferguson was spending part of his summer holiday watching football, scouting, whether for players or ideas. It was the cause of much frivolity among journalistic colleagues that I almost literally bumped into him. I think we were both taken by surprise but I took the lead, suggesting that we put the past behind us and start the new season with the slate wiped clean. But it was clear he wasn't interested, so I walked off.

Little did I know but Colin Gibson and Steve Curry, then the football correspondents of the *Daily Telegraph* and the *Daily Express*, and good friends of mine, casually dropped into their subsequent conversation with Alex that I was celebrating my fortieth birthday that very day. Wouldn't it be a good idea for us all to have a bottle of bubbly or two down by the lakeside?

Ferguson duly turned up. Gibson and Curry believed it was a grand gesture of reconciliation on his part, but I always sensed he was smiling through gritted teeth. Nothing that has happened since has altered my opinion.

Basically, after that, I lost all interest in making up. Whatever he did, it would not change my view that anything I said or wrote, provided it was honest and true, amounted to fair comment. But there was one last occasion where I thought, we're both getting on in years, this is daft . . .

I was asked to give an interview to the *Glasgow Evening Herald*. It was conducted over lunch at Mottram Hall, a few miles from where I live, and a favourite haunt of Ferguson's. Inevitably, the question of Fergie and me came up. I was expecting it and thought I handled it quite well. 'That's long in the past,' I said. 'I'm sure he thinks about it no more than I do. I know I have great respect for his achievements as a manager even if we're not likely to have dinner together!'

I wrote to Alex telling him about the interview and asking, once and for all, for us to shelve our differences. What a shame, I suggested, that two people who care so much for the game couldn't respect each other. We didn't have to socialise, I told him, but if we held a civilised conversation then it would be much less likely that I would misunderstand anything that he did. I might disagree, but I wouldn't misinterpret.

A fortnight later, Alex wrote his reply:

Dear Mr Green,
I acknowledge receipt of your correspondence of the 29th October 1997, and note your comments.
    However, I have said all I wish to regarding Radio 5 Live, and all those associated with that programme [sic].

Yours sincerely,

Alex Ferguson CBE
MANAGER

It wasn't even signed.

Alex is an enormously successful manager, deserving to be rated alongside the greats in the British game like Busby, Bob Paisley, Bill

Shankly, Don Revie and Jock Stein. As a human being, though, I wouldn't give him the time of day. He is, in my experience, foul-mouthed and arrogant, and does not like to be crossed. Presumably he resents my forthright approach, preferring journalists who are more sycophantic.

I have great sympathy for some of those journalists, as many are friends. They need access to what the manager of Manchester United says and thinks, either to sell their newspapers or to fill their local radio station output. But I have seen Ferguson yell at individuals in front of their colleagues and get away with it. I remember one occasion at Elland Road where Jimmy Armfield was on the receiving end and said he felt humiliated.

John Motson still shudders at the thought of one such confrontation with the United boss at Old Trafford after Manchester United had played Middlesbrough and Roy Keane had been sent off for an altercation with Jan Aage Fjortoft.

On a Saturday, television commentators might find themselves doing two interviews with the same person, one live for *Grandstand*, the other recorded for *Match of the Day*. Now Motson is no Jeremy Paxman, and when Ferguson dismissed his mild question regarding Keane's behaviour, John left the matter alone. Brian Barwick, now Head of Sport for ITV but then in charge of the BBC's football output, spoke to Motson before the second interview and pressed him to push Ferguson on the subject. Unhappily, John obliged, though only in the gentlest manner. Unfortunately, Ferguson went crazy, pulled off his lapel microphone and launched into Motson, and the BBC in general, implying that many were fully paid-up members of the Liverpool supporters' club. In the interests of balance, I should point out that Barwick comes from Liverpool and that the BBC employs Alan Hansen and Mark Lawrenson. So what?

News of the row couldn't be covered up. We heard about it

in the press room shortly afterwards and later I was aware of the disagreement that ensued in the *Match of the Day* office. Though Ferguson had thrown his microphone away and walked out of shot of the camera, every word had been recorded. Des Lynam was in favour of it being broadcast, suitably 'bleeped', to show this different side of Ferguson, but others were against. Sadly, the others won.

I don't know what goes on in Ferguson's head, but he appears to me to be a control freak. When suggestions were made to Martin Edwards that United's appalling PR could do with some spin-doctoring and a genuinely influential press officer, the former chief executive always responded by making it clear that his manager did not want this. No, I'm afraid the emergence of Manchester United Radio and Manchester United TV suits the manager perfectly. You'll have to search hard to detect any criticism in their output. I appreciate that such coverage meets the needs of those who are completely blinkered in their support for the club. However, I wouldn't accept that it's anything other than club propaganda.

After the 1998 European Cup final, I ran into Brian Kidd at Amsterdam airport on the way home. Brian was still Ferguson's number two. He hadn't yet moved to Blackburn Rovers. We had a long and friendly chat and Brian asked me to explain to him why there was such antipathy between Alex and me. As best I could, I gave him the background. All he could do was shake his head.

Ironically, and very sadly, Kidd has since learnt to his own cost what happens if Ferguson decides to attack. Ferguson's dismissal in his autobiography of someone he once termed as 'like a brother' was a disgrace. Brian just didn't see the attack coming.

I suppose if it were merely a case of two individuals not liking each other, you could say, what's the harm? Unfortunately, there have been times when I've felt that Ferguson seems to have made life potentially difficult for me. He's even quoted me as a reason for refusing to talk to 5 Live.

During the summer of 1997, stories appeared in some newspapers suggesting that Ferguson was trying to persuade the League Managers' Association to have me 'banned', whatever that was supposed to mean, though the LMA denied this.

It has even filtered through to the fans. Because of our differences articles have also been written in various Manchester United fanzines, most completely fabricated in terms of the stories that they purport to tell, that made me the target of verbal abuse and physical threat when I visited Old Trafford. It wasn't at all pleasant. You wouldn't believe the response I get when United fans, who've assumed that I'm the enemy, meet the real me.

Of more lasting damage, I'm certain that the well-publicised dispute between the two of us must have, at least partially, dissuaded anyone who thought I might become a television commentator. Ferguson intimidates as many broadcasting executives as he does journalists. I'm sure I'm perceived as a problem they can do without.

Nowadays, I'm happy to ignore Ferguson knowing that I'm able to carry on doing my job without having to tolerate his behaviour. Pity those who can't, like Martin Samuel, the outstanding football writer on the *Daily Express*. In typical fashion, Manchester United made a public relations disaster of their trip to Rio de Janeiro for the inaugural FIFA Club World Championship. When a little forethought might have had an adoring Brazilian public eating out of their hands, United initially chose to lock the locals away from their training sessions. Worse, they repelled the approaches of the Brazilian media, who are accustomed to having full and free access to their own international stars. By the time of the first official press conference, United had already lost the PR contest.

At first, Ferguson handled it really well, responding diplomatically to every question, even the odd 'daisy-cutter'. However, at the close, everyone noticed, even if they couldn't quite overhear, a brief confrontation with Samuel. The reporter, like all of us frustrated at United's previous lack of communication, had inadvertently mis-quoted the manager on the advice of a third party. Ferguson was now communicating his feelings on the matter.

The red mist had descended. Ignoring the continuing presence of the world's media, and the rolling television cameras, Ferguson swore at Samuel. Now, Martin isn't one to be intimidated by threatening behaviour. He rightly fought his corner, at which Ferguson became even more heated. It was a pathetic performance from one of the leading figures in world football.

Maybe his football achievements should shunt all other consider-ations to one side. I'm told Bill Shankly and Jock Stein were both men that it was best not to cross. And Matt Busby's withering silences disguised a cut-throat manner when he deemed it necessary. You'll notice, all of them Scots. Yet I don't think Ferguson's magnificence as a manager can excuse his behaviour.

Bluntly, he is someone I'd have preferred not to have to deal with. When he retires, if he retires, as the last of a certain breed, football will undoubtedly miss him. But I won't. I'll toast his departure.

CHAPTER THREE

WHO RUNS THE GAME?

Who runs football? FIFA? In the European arena, UEFA? Domestically, the Football Association? Even a decade ago I wouldn't have hesitated to say yes to all three but how things have changed in that decade.

Football is now run by its major clubs not by its authorities. Oh, those authorities can huff and puff and issue all sorts of threats but, ultimately, they'll back down for fear of the clubs taking up their toys and going off somewhere else to play.

I really had no inkling of what was afoot when I attended a meeting of the FA Council in 1991 in Torquay. There was a rumour that many of the First Division clubs were ready to revolt and quit the Football League to form their own organisation. That rumour quickly, and unexpectedly, became fact. I hadn't met Rick Parry before I was invited, along with other journalists, up to his hotel room to be informed that the leading clubs had tendered their resignation from the League. It was a clever pre-emptive strike that forced the hand of the Football Association.

Suddenly, the FA, football's governing body in this country, moved swiftly in an attempt to keep the big clubs on board. There'd be a new Premiership, linked through promotion and relegation to the Football League, but separate in organisation and status. It would be the 'FA Premiership', but no one was in any doubt as to who was in charge . . . the clubs. Really, it was the FA that was trying to stay on board, giving the clubs what they wanted under the guise of retaining control.

Still in doubt? Remember the FA's blueprint for the future? It envisaged cutting the top division from twenty-two clubs to eighteen, and ideally sixteen. This would leave England at the top of football's pyramid structure with everything geared to the success of the national side. That was the idea anyway. The reality? Kevin Keegan eschewed the opportunity to arrange important friendly fixtures in March and April 2000 before the European Championship knowing that he'd be wasting his time. Such games would annoy the clubs, whose priorities lay elsewhere, and the national coach would find he had skeleton, under-strength squads to work with as players withdrew for various spurious reasons. There was no point.

And the size of the Premiership? Well, we got down to twenty, but that's it. It is certainly in the interests of the national team, and the game generally, not least the players, to have fewer fixtures but which Premiership clubs will, in effect, vote themselves off the gravy train? None. Only Manchester United and Arsenal would vote consistently for a reduction in the size of the Premiership, but then they vote from a position of strength. Neither club is conceivably threatened by relegation.

I almost feel sorry for the FA, so weakened is their role, but then I see how they react in other circumstances and my sympathy drains away. Take the FA Cup. Who doubts that it has been the greatest cup competition of all time? However, the harm inflicted on that marvellous tournament in recent years, presided over by the FA, may have caused telling and lasting damage.

Manchester United should never have been allowed to withdraw in 1999–2000 to fulfil a commitment to play in the FIFA Club World Championship. I don't care if United's absence from Brazil might have affected England's bid to host the 2006 World Cup, a theory I have severe doubts about anyway. United should have been told to field a team, any team. The club, after all, hasn't shied away from selecting weakened line-ups in the League Cup. Nobody has punished them for that. So, field a team. Or United could have had their fourth-round tie delayed. Or they could have entered the tournament at a later stage. I had no problem with United playing in Brazil. They were also trailblazers in the mid-fifties when they defied the Football League and entered the European Cup. Look where that led. I have few doubts that the Club World Championship will, ultimately, be a similar success. But to excuse the holders from the need to defend the FA Cup was inexcusable and the Football Association was to blame. Not United.

The FA is guilty on other counts, too, of demeaning its own great competition: cutting back on replays, even cutting them out altogether, as is the case now with the semi-finals; moving the third round to December – a horrible mistake that they have at least acknowledged and corrected; and playing semi-finals on different dates at Wembley.

However, there is a pattern to all these decisions. It's about keeping the big clubs happy. Giving them room to fulfil their commitments in Europe and elsewhere. Caving in to their requests as opposed to meeting the responsibilities of an organisation that's meant to supervise the game for the benefit of the whole. The Football Association is weak, the clubs are strong, particularly some clubs.

Look at how they deal with discipline – a fair deal for all? One of the most unappetising sights of 1999–2000 was the horrendous verbal assault on referee Andy d'Urso by Manchester United players after he had the effrontery to award a penalty to Middlesbrough at Old Trafford – an event that even provoked Alex Ferguson into a rare public criticism of his players. What happened? Nothing. The pathetic excuse offered was that d'Urso hadn't mentioned the incident in his report. So what? The whole of the nation saw what happened on television that evening. On other occasions, the FA acts on video evidence. Why not on this one? Is the argument correct that the FA is frightened to take on Manchester United? Is that why David Elleray went for so long without officiating at a United match? Merely because, rightly or wrongly, he had sent off Denis Irwin in a key fixture at Anfield?

The FA talks tough about discipline but inflicts punishment with a feather duster. United got away with the d'Urso business. Leeds and Tottenham were fined after some rank bad behaviour at Elland Road (I thought Spurs were largely blameless anyway). Fined? I'm sure the club accountants were quaking in their boots. The FA shouldn't talk about deducting points in such circumstances, it should get on with it.

Have no doubts. The Premiership clubs run football in England, not the FA. They run the key division and their decisions affect football at all levels. If only most of them could see the bigger picture and redistribute even a fraction more of their riches to the parts of the game that so badly need help. But they won't. Great equals Greed in our game.

Of course, the Football Association isn't alone in its struggles. Pity poor UEFA as well. Do you think that UEFA developed the Champions League as it has done because the Swiss-based governing body truly felt it was the path to follow? Not a chance. UEFA brought us a quasi-European League because they knew if they didn't do it, Europe's biggest clubs would do it for them and leave UEFA in charge only of a rump.

There is a significant body of clubs called the Group of Fourteen. They include Manchester United and Liverpool and they meet regularly among themselves. They also meet regularly with UEFA. Now you'd think that UEFA might try putting this group in its place, telling them *we* run the game in Europe, not you. It doesn't because it can't. The reverse is true. Just as the FA recognises that clubs rule the roost in England so, too, does UEFA in Europe.

What's been happening in the transformation of the European Cup into what is now the Champions (sic) League is the desperate act of an organisation, UEFA, trying to retain a measure of control. If the clubs want a Champions League that has three group stages, UEFA will implement it. If they wish to revert to one instead of two, and increase the number of clubs in each group, UEFA will do that as well. UEFA will do anything to prevent the clubs breaking away and doing their own thing.

To be fair, both the FA and UEFA have national interests at heart as well. They want to retain international football. If they can stay in control then the clubs won't entirely smother the Englands and the Spains and the Italys. Make no mistake, that's the trend. Ask any fan of any leading club – what's more important, your club winning or your country? It's no contest, is it?

It's ironic then that FIFA, whose interests are overwhelmingly with international football, have clearly looked from afar at the importance and the influence of the UEFA Champions League and decided that they want a piece of the action as well. Hence the Club World Championship.

The sceptics were scathing about the first tournament in Brazil and it's undeniable that there were problems with the weather, the venues and the influence of television in deciding kick-off times and format. Then there was the question of the presence of some clubs and the absence of others. Yet, throughout, I felt I was observing the start of something big, an idea that would grow and develop and, in time, become as important as the European Cup but on a global stage.

However, it raises important questions, similar questions to those posed about the Champions League. Where are we heading? How much will European and global ambitions be to the detriment of domestic competition? I'm tempted to believe overwhelmingly so.

How would Manchester United list their priorities? The League Cup? Obviously they hardly think about a competition where they are happy to field reserve elevens. The FA Cup? No one forced them to withdraw and no one can tell me that the board at Old Trafford wasn't eyeing up the vast commercial opportunities presented by playing in Rio. The Championship? After winning the Premiership title six times in the first eight years of its existence, and being runners-up on the other two occasions, the glory of taking that prize must be diminishing, though the players show no sign of it as yet. No, even for United fans, it's the Champions League that matters most now. That's why the 1999–2000 Premiership title felt like mere consolation for losing to Real Madrid at the quarter-final stage of Europe's Holy Grail.

The club is so big, so successful, it looks far beyond domestic considerations. Europe dominates everything in its vicinity. For all of us. From mid-September 1999 to April 2000, Leeds United, playing some superb football, were never lower than second in the Premiership, yet not once in that period did I get to go to Elland Road. It wasn't out of choice. Producers and editors choose my games, not me. It was simply that I was so busy with the Champions League, every foreign trip taking up three days of my week. I was at the Nou Camp three times as often that season as I was at Elland Road.

And even for commentators, as no doubt for players, the domestic fixtures lost an edge. If I've been in Barcelona or in Madrid on Wednesday night, a game at Villa Park or at the Riverside Stadium isn't going to seem as attractive. How can it be? It's only natural. Domestic football is suffering.

How to redress the balance? I wish I knew. This European rollercoaster is relentless, smothering so many of the things that we used to take for granted. How we preferred to see Arsenal against Spurs instead of Arsenal against Ajax. How we loved the third round of the FA Cup, no matter who was playing, and wouldn't have allowed anything else to get in the way – like going to Rio instead.

Once again, football's greed for growth and money is taking us away from the grass roots, from the considerations that made the game great in the first place. It's time that the authorities paid much more attention to what the fans think and more time to safeguarding their interests.

I think I know much of what you all think because I'm a fan as well. We're all fed up with the influence that television has. We get angry that Leeds and Arsenal can play in the semi-finals of the UEFA Cup and you can see them only on Sky Digital. We see players as greedy and the clubs as greedier still. There seems to be no end to price rises for tickets and shirts, indeed for everything. And no one cares when we complain. They know if it's not you or me, there'll be someone else willing to fork out the cash.

The list of our complaints and gripes is endless. The problem is, unfortunately, football's governing bodies, the Football Association, UEFA, FIFA, are so heavily engaged in their struggle to stay in charge, they can hardly spare the time to deal with our problems. At least that's how it seems. Moreover, we can't even be sure that their interests are still the same as ours. And if you're hoping that they can stem the influence of the biggest clubs, or even want to, I truly fear that you're wasting your time.

CHAPTER FOUR

IRRITATING OTHERS . . .

K enny Dalglish and I now get on fine together. It wasn't always so. Yet, thinking back, I still can't quite understand why.

If you were to ask me who is the best British player I've ever seen, unquestionably it's Dalglish. Alan Hansen is the best defender but all round, definitely Dalglish.

I know you're asking, why not George Best? Unfortunately, to my great regret, I only ever saw George play once in the flesh. That was at Windsor Park in Belfast for Northern Ireland against Scotland in 1967. George beat the Scots on his own that day, even if Eric McMordie scored the only goal. McMordie had been a colleague of Best when they first appeared at Old Trafford, fresh-faced and promising, from Belfast. Both were inordinately homesick and quickly returned to Northern Ireland. It was as well for Manchester United that Best had a rethink. Eric chose a different footballing career, one that proved not nearly as successful as George's. 'Bestie' must have been absolutely fabulous and I do envy those who watched him regularly from the

Stretford End. My view was through television and newspapers.

But Kenny was someone that I did see regularly from close quarters. Though slight of build, he looked to me to have everything. Most important, he had ability: a sureness of passing, clinical finishing but, above all, the awareness of others that separates the merely good from the great. I will never forget the deftness of touch and the vision with which Dalglish set up a marvellous goal for Ian Rush one afternoon at Anfield. Actually, many goals, many afternoons.

Dalglish is never one for a wasted word. He chooses carefully who he speaks to and what he talks about. As a BBC reporter in the early to mid-eighties, I hung on his every utterance. I was in the presence of a legend. I could only learn.

Above all, I respected Kenny Dalglish. So it shook me to my foundations to discover that I had crossed him. By this stage, he was manager of Blackburn Rovers, and a very fine one, even if praise has to be tempered with the knowledge that it was the fortunes of Jack Walker that were backing Dalglish's judgement. Kenny had led the club into the Premiership and, for the first time in the history of one of the founder clubs of the Football League, into European competition, the UEFA Cup.

They didn't do well. They lost to the might of the Swedish part-time outfit, Trelleborg, or as the doyen of British football journalism, David Lacey of the *Guardian*, put it: 'The Trelleborg Chamber of Commerce.'

Fully four months after the ignominy of this two-legged defeat, I went to Ewood Park for a replayed FA Cup tie against Newcastle United. Kenny had been sidelined for some weeks through appendicitis, so his presence was unexpected. I was collecting my ticket at reception when I saw Kenny across the foyer, looking thin and drawn after his illness. I approached him: 'How are you, Kenny? Feeling any better?'

'I'm fine. Better than your commentary,' he replied. 'You'll never be forgiven for what you said the night of the Trelleborg game.'

'What are you talking about?'

'You said my team was a waste of money. You'll never be forgiven.'

'Kenny, how long have you known me? I never say anything I don't believe. I've never thought your team was a waste of money, therefore I didn't say it. What I might have said that night was that there would be people watching who might *think* your team was a waste of money, not being able to beat Trelleborg. That's different. Anyway, I thought you were coaching the side from the dugout. How do you know what I said?' Kenny walked away and when I tried to follow him a steward restrained me. I was very angry.

In Kenny's autobiography, I was one of only two journalists that he named, in derogatory terms. I checked and could have sued, but it wasn't worth it. Truth is, I like the guy. I'm not sure he ever accepted that I didn't say what he thought I said, or what he was told I said, but it hardly matters. Kenny is good and Kenny cares. So do I.

Joe Royle is perhaps even more sensitive. I first came across Joe at Oldham and I can't begin to tell you how highly I regarded him. Not only did he seem the most approachable of managers, he was in charge of the most beautiful of Cinderella clubs. Oldham, on the surface, didn't have a lot going for it. I always thought Boundary Park was the coldest possible venue for commentary, even in May or August, yet it had the heartiest of welcomes. I loved going there.

Perhaps I was blinded initially by the welcome of the place to the football that the team played under Royle. Only when he went to Everton, narrowly avoiding the England job along the way, did I see what Royle's brand of football represented. To keep that club safe from relegation, Royle promoted a scrapping long-ball style, as far removed from the 'School of Science' approach beloved at Goodison as you could possibly find. Trouble is, it continued after relegation was averted. True Evertonians hated it, and Royle left.

I next encountered him in Sofia in 1999, a few days after his new team, Manchester City, had won promotion to the First Division having beaten Gillingham in a play-off at Wembley. I had been commentating on the game and, with due respect to the Kent outfit, I was really pleased. Without any affiliation to the team, I had always found City a great club to deal with and wished them well.

I saw Joe in the hotel reception area as he was checking in. He was working for Channel 5 that afternoon, I was on 5 Live. I had my hand outstretched. 'I don't know what your problem is with the BBC [I'd been aware that Royle had been more than awkward with the BBC in recent months] but I just want to say congrat—' I didn't get any further.

'You're the problem. You slaughtered me when I was at Everton. Slaughtered me!'

'No, Joe,' I replied, 'I didn't slaughter you, I slaughtered the football the team was playing. So, too, did the Evertonians I spoke to.'

I see hardly any First Division football so I didn't catch up with City's campaign for promotion the following season until their home game against Charlton who, by that stage, were almost certain of promotion themselves. I was looking forward to a rare visit to Maine Road.

Unfortunately, it was a terrible game and I didn't spare any blushes. Out loud, during the commentary, I wondered how many players in the City line-up were of Premiership quality. I suggested perhaps no more than one or two. My summariser, David Fairclough, went further. He described Robert Taylor as a 'pub player'. Royle, no doubt, would have been steaming enough about what I said, but his anger would have increased when some newspapers mistakenly attributed the quote about Taylor to me.

Royle should have brushed aside any criticism as merely the

opinion of others, which it was. He didn't. Instead, he complained about me in the media. I could stand that but, sadly, Royle's attitude was picked up by many City fans. Their ridiculous notion that I am a United fan now seems to step over the line into marking me out as a City enemy. Neither is true, and it is particularly ironic given that United fans are equally convinced I'm hostile to their club. Hopefully, if Joe actually listens to what I say or reads what I write, normal relations will be resumed as soon as possible.

I'd be lying if I didn't admit that I, too, am sensitive to criticism. Who isn't? However, you can get by when you don't confuse personal and professional criticism. Patently, Royle does. Someone like Martin O'Neill doesn't. We have known each other for a very long while. I first met him when he was about to appear for Nottingham Forest in the European Cup final and I was working as a television reporter in Belfast. I persuaded the news editor that Martin was worth doing a lengthy feature on. Martin is a great talker and is so popular that lots of people like to talk about him. The item turned out to be nearly half the length of the programme.

Naturally, I have followed his progress into management with personal as well as professional interest and you won't be surprised to hear that I have vigorously applauded his success at Leicester City that earned him the big job at Celtic in the summer of 2000. But I won't allow that to cloud my judgement. For example, while he was there however much I admired Leicester City as a club, easily among the most helpful and welcoming in the country, with great supporters, it didn't stop me sometimes criticising how they played. Like at the 1997 League Cup final against Middlesbrough.

The first meeting at Wembley was so awful, both Mike Ingham and I winced at the thought of describing the replay at Hillsborough. If anything, the second game was even worse. I remember the look on Mike's face as we neared the end of normal time: it spelt horror sensing another thirty minutes of such drivel lay ahead.

Now, I perfectly understand how the fans of both sides might have been entirely unaware of how poor the football was. Their team was in a final and all they really cared about was that their team won. Neutral observers must be free to view things from a more dispassionate stance, to see the game for what it is.

Afterwards, Steve May interviewed Martin, who was delighted beyond words at Leicester winning the trophy and qualifying for European football for the first time. Towards the end of their conversation – I was listening from the commentary position high up in the main stand – May (a Leicester fan himself) sheepishly suggested that some observers had thought it wasn't much of a spectacle. Martin said he was surprised that anyone had felt that way. 'Actually,' said May, 'it was Alan Green who thought it was awful.' At this, Martin balked audibly: 'I can't believe that. I'm really disappointed in Alan. How could he think that?'

I was absolutely furious to be dragged into it and later let May know precisely what I thought of him.

A few days after the final, I wrote to Martin. I stood by my view of the match and hoped that he would one day be able to watch the video and see it more as it looked to me.

Martin's a really bright guy. He knows his football and is no fool. A short while later, I saw him at the annual Football Writers' Dinner and we had a good laugh about the affair.

Nevertheless, he would have been aware that I've also felt moved to criticise some of Leicester's football since then. I remember doing commentary on City against Wimbledon at Filbert Street the night that the former nanny, Louise Woodward, was due to hear her fate at the hands of a Boston judge. Radio 5 Live wouldn't leave the news story for the football until the verdict was announced. Thank heavens!

It was among the worst games I've ever seen.

The truth is Martin did an incredible job with scant resources. That he achieved a secure Premiership future for Leicester, and won trophies, deserves the highest praise. But that didn't make them pretty to watch. Too often they resembled a faintly better Wimbledon. I'm delighted that Martin has taken on a really big club in Celtic and I'll bet the football his team play will be rather easier to watch. Meantime, I hope he understood and forgave the odd critical remark from an old and dear friend.

Speaking of Wimbledon, am I in such a minority disliking the way that club plays the game? When they only just escaped relegation in 1999, I left wondering just who would have bothered attending the funeral. The following year we found out. Of course, I appreciated the romantic nature of their rags-to-riches history – for a while. It quickly wore off watching their approach to football. I used to treasure the seasons that I'd go through without having to see them play more than once or twice. Or better, not at all.

I reckon they escaped the wrath of the general public only because of some of the truly nice people that have been manager there, like Dave Bassett and Bobby Gould, both of whom it is impossible not to like and admire. Now, you may be wondering why I don't include Joe Kinnear in that group. The omission is deliberate.

I don't know what it is about Kinnear. I accept that, generally, he's very popular but he isn't with me. People say that Wimbledon's football was becoming more attractive when he was in charge. I didn't notice any difference. It was as ugly as it ever was. The Crazy Gang wasn't fun in your face. It was aggressive and intimidating, and it was meant to be. Kinnear was part of that. It makes me wonder why so many clubs have been rumoured to be interested in him since he left Selhurst Park. Do they want to play in that way?

Kinnear turned down various invitations to appear on my Friday evening programme. Why the producers persisted in asking, I didn't know. Anyway, Karen Barber, who was in charge of the programme during season 1998–99, finally got a 'yes' from the Wimbledon boss. He agreed to attend a special New Year's Day edition which was to be recorded a couple of days beforehand. I was sceptical but Karen reassured me. He seemed very enthusiastic about appearing, and to ease my continuing concerns, she made frequent calls to Kinnear in the weeks leading up to the show, merely making an excuse to check that he was still on board.

Everything seemed fixed. The day of the recording, I sat in the office at Television Centre. There was an hour and a half left before we were due to start. The phone rang. It was Kinnear's secretary, who was practically in tears. She was new to the job and said she'd never had to do anything like this before: Joe wasn't coming. He'd stayed up in Yorkshire following the previous night's game against Leeds, apparently to look at a player. He surely knew the difficulties involved in finding a late replacement on such a day for a programme like that. It was a miracle that I was able to get hold of the Crystal Palace manager, Steve Coppell, who came in instead at ridiculously short notice, and was far better than Kinnear would have been.

Since then, another Friday night producer, Rob Smith, has twice suggested inviting Kinnear on as a guest. He obviously forgot my response first time around: 'By all means, ask him. But you'll have to get a new presenter if he says yes.'

CHAPTER FIVE

GETTING IT RIGHT – AND WRONG

I n the 1998–99 Champions Cup semi-final in Turin, Manchester United recovered from going 2–0 down in the first ten minutes to beat Juventus and win on Italian soil for the first time in their history. United's third goal that night in the Stadio Delle Alpi was scored by Andy Cole, after a run by Dwight Yorke.

Mike Ingham, the BBC's football correspondent, was alongside me and was commentating at the time. Initially, he gave the goal to Yorke. Neither I nor the summariser involved, Mark Lawrenson, could understand why. Both of us were sure it was Cole. Yes, Yorke had been involved. His run into the penalty area had wreaked havoc in the Juventus defence and when he was fouled, the ball broke to Cole who forced it over the line.

Mike's reaction mid-move was the same as ours: that there must be a penalty. He looked to the linesman expecting him to flag and in that instant, Cole scored. When Mike glanced back towards the goalmouth he wrongly assumed that Yorke had regained his footing and had somehow managed to finish the move.

Now this is the kind of error that happens to all commentators, but Mike was mortified. I understood. To begin with, I know of no one more dedicated than he is to getting it right. That doesn't mean that Mike is fussy, merely that he works very hard to ensure mistakes are kept to an absolute minimum. This one hurt. It was such a vital fixture. The commentary clip on such a crucial moment was certainly destined to be retained in the BBC archives.

Worse, he felt that in his confusion over the goalscorer some, mischievously or otherwise, might interpret the error as having racist overtones. Here, he was both right and wrong. Wrong, in that it is easy to mix up players whatever their colour. To this day, I don't know how I credited a Crystal Palace goal at Selhurst Park to Mark Bright when the scorer was Geoff Thomas! I remember, too, when Ian Rush returned to Liverpool, after a season at Juventus, how I couldn't tell him apart from John Aldridge. Their appearance was very similar. Both had moustaches. They ran in the same way. Their predatory instincts had them arriving in the penalty box at the same time and usually in the same spot. Come to think of it, Rush and Aldridge, brilliant goalscorers though they were, weren't the ideal partnership for Liverpool. They were also a commentator's nightmare.

Where Mike was right, unfortunately, is that someone did send a letter in virtually accusing him of being a racist. I encouraged Mike to tear it up as I felt that if he replied it would be giving credence to an accusation that was totally without foundation. Mike finally agreed. The funny thing is, only a few weeks later, I momentarily confused Yorke with Cole and with far less excuse.

Commentators do have excuses, at least on radio where it's unusual to have a television monitor to check what might be difficult through normal vision. I can't tell you why, because it doesn't make any sense whatsoever, but radio people frequently find themselves in the worst possible seats as far as the media is concerned. Our television counterparts are pampered to the Nth degree and the print journalists have traditionally held centre stage. Not so the radio interlopers.

It was with enormous relief that I sat down in my commentary position for the 1999 European Cup final in Barcelona. It was directly over the halfway line and within reasonable distance of the playing surface. Normally, radio commentators at the Nou Camp find themselves over a corner flag and so high up in that magnificent stadium that they're almost touching the clouds. I suffered badly there one evening commentating on Barcelona against Manchester United. It was in October, there was mist swirling around the ground and United were in an unfamiliar white strip. I was so far away from the action I might have been commentating on Subbuteo and the only player I recognised was Ray Wilkins. Even then Ray was losing his hair and I could easily spot his bald pate.

I'm not exaggerating. United, defending the goal to my left in the first half, were at least two hundred yards from where I was sitting. I was doing what we call 'stop-start commentary'. In other words, I would begin to commentate if I felt something of significance was going to happen. It would be recorded in London and played in later if necessary.

Barcelona took a corner and the ball deflected into the net off the head of a United defender whom I identified, somewhat shakily, as Graeme Hogg. He was making his European debut for the club. However, I was far from certain and immediately I rounded off the clip I told the studio that I wasn't sure it had been Hogg.

My summariser, Jimmy Armfield, didn't help. 'No, Alan, it was Kevin Moran.' I wasn't certain that Jim was right either. I leant towards the adjoining commentary box where the injured Gordon McQueen was working for a local radio station. 'Who got it?' I asked.

'Arnold Muhren,' he said. Now, I thought, McQueen should know, he plays in the team.

Anyway, it was impossible to check the facts before I started commentating for real during the second half. Instead, I employed the classic commentary fudge: 'I thought the own goal was Hogg's but others think it was Moran's or Muhren's. What I am certain of, and it's all Manchester United will care about, is that they're a goal down here in Barcelona.'

I still didn't know half an hour after the game ended. United had lost 2–0. I stood outside the team coach plucking up the courage to ask someone who was guilty of scoring the own goal. Hogg came towards the bus. He was crying. I didn't need to ask.

People assume identification is among the most difficult tasks of the commentator's trade and, sure enough, sometimes circumstances dictate that it is. Your view might be poor. It might be non-existent, as at Scarborough when they played Arsenal in a League Cup tie. I arrived at the McCain Stadium fully expecting the game to be postponed. The area was shrouded in dense fog. The drive across the Pennines to the east coast was crazy. I kept telling myself that I shouldn't be wasting my time and should turn around and go back home.

It was still two hours before kick-off. I could hardly see a turnstile to negotiate. To start a match in these conditions would be farcical. Never mind the difficulties for commentators, what about the punters who paid to come in? Wasn't it reasonable that they should be able to see the game?

Technically, the referee is within his rights to begin a match if he can stand on the halfway line and see both goals. This referee decided that he could, surely a case of the blind leading the blind.

Brian Rix should have been playing. The master of the Whitehall Theatre would have had wonderful material to play with. There was but one moment in the entire game when the fog lifted. Mercifully, that was the moment in which Nigel Winterburn scored the only goal. It came during Mike Ingham's period of commentary. I saw nothing during mine. I was reduced to 'assuming that Arsenal have the ball because there are some yellow shirts [their away strip] moving from right to left'. I kid you not! When people ask me if I am ever worried that I'll find nothing to talk about, I tell them: 'No. I was at Scarborough in the fog!'

Mostly, I am commentating on teams that I see frequently. For example, I might watch Arsenal, Chelsea, Liverpool or Manchester United thirty or forty times a season. If I can't recognise those players, I really should retire from commentary. Generally, I know both teams but if there's one that I'm less familiar with, say Wimbledon or Southampton, I'm sure to know the other and that will help take any pressure off. You always find, within a few minutes of the game starting, that you've spotted that X runs in a particular way, that Y is bald and that Z has his shirt outside his shorts. It really isn't difficult and any commentator who tells you otherwise is trying to persuade you that he's better than he probably is.

Of course, delving into European competition or a World Cup is entirely another matter. No matter how experienced a commentator is, it's unsettling to talk about players that you've never seen before and know nothing about. When you await a European draw or you're handed a World Cup schedule, believe me, your enthusiasm is greatly affected by the teams involved. Seeing Manchester United in the Champions League is something to dread if they're away to Lodz. Watching Holland in Marseille during France 98 has the edge taken off it if they are playing South Korea. In these cases, I try not to panic. I know I'm bound to make mistakes so I think, don't be afraid to admit them. Have a laugh at your own expense. I think that the listener likes to be reminded that his commentator is occasionally vulnerable and is also humble enough to acknowledge if he's got it wrong.

You know, before a World Cup, which countries will provide the most problems. Japan, Korea, Iran, Morocco . . . those you don't know and find it difficult to tell apart. Racial characteristics comes into it but, believe me, it's not racist. I remember flying to Stockholm for the opening match in the 1992 European Championship. Rob Hawthorne, who now works for Sky Sports but was then in BBC Radio, was doing the game with me. We decided to go to watch Sweden train. I was half expecting to see twenty-two identically built blond footballers emerge from the tunnel at the Rasunda Stadium.

I almost yelled for joy when the first player ran on to the pitch. I already knew him but he had the number 10 on the back of his shirt with the name BROLIN emblazoned above it. There could be no mistake. Heck, I thought, this is the first time I've even seen players wearing names and numbers during a training session. What a cinch! Unfortunately, my joy evaporated almost immediately when the rest of the squad came out, all wearing number 10, all named BROLIN!

Every commentator has his own way of preparing for games. Some will study photographs or videos, assuming they have the time to do so. Usually, we in radio don't have the time. 'That's one game over and it's straight on to the next.' I commentated on seven games in the first nine days of that European Championship in Sweden and no two consecutive matches were in the same city. Preparation? I barely had time to sleep.

I'm happy to go and observe and react; I'm an impulsive commentator. I'll never burden listeners with a list of statistics or clever phrases, partly because I'm too lazy to put in the effort required, mostly because I don't believe that's the best way for me to broadcast.

★　★　★

Like every commentator, I worry about declining eyesight. How can you call it if you don't see it? Age does take its toll on everyone's health. Years of wearing headphones at incredibly noisy outside broadcasts has definitely had a detrimental effect on my hearing. My wife thinks I should sue the BBC and retire on the proceeds. It's probably too late for that. I console myself with the knowledge that Mike Ingham's hearing is infinitely worse than mine!

Years ago I began to notice that on midwinter nights in dodgy commentary positions, particularly if the floodlights weren't good, I was having difficulty spotting players at distance. I put it down to tiredness but made a mental note to have my eyesight checked at the end of the season.

I went along to a local optician's in Macclesfield. They confirmed that my vision had lost a little of its sharpness and that I would have to wear glasses. Nothing to worry about, they said: 'You're just getting old, Greenie.' However, something else had shown up in their tests and they thought I'd best see my GP, just to be certain. He referred me to Macclesfield General Hospital.

As a matter of course, I went along. I wasn't really concerned. I still felt my vision was A1, or near as damn it. I attended the clinic of a Mr Gupta. He put in drops that blurred my vision and carefully put a lens directly on to each eye. I noticed that he wasn't saying a great deal. Suddenly, he announced: 'You have glaucoma, Mr Green. I want you to take these drops that I will prescribe for you. Three of each, in each eye, four times a day, and I want you back here in a week's time. I'll decide what to do then.'

I must have left the hospital in a state of shock. I hadn't even asked what glaucoma was and what it would do to me. I got to the car and thought it best to go the library so that I could look up the term in a medical dictionary. I soon wished that I hadn't. I read: 'Glaucoma causes 40% of the cases of blindness in the United Kingdom. Its progress can be arrested but it cannot be cured.'

I stumbled through the front door of my house. In my ignorance, fuelled by a few words in a dictionary, I thought my career and my whole way of life was over. How would I work? How would I support my family? What was happening to me? I broke down and cried.

A week later, I returned to see Mr Gupta. He wasn't happy. The drops weren't working. The pressure around my eyes, caused by the inability of the fluid to drain away, wasn't going down. Glaucoma is a terrible chronic illness. Some of its most severe damage, to the optic nerves, is done before the sufferer knows anything about it. If I hadn't gone for the eye test, and the problem was undiscovered for much longer, I would have been in very serious trouble. As it was, Mr Gupta was worried. He drastically increased the dosage of the drops and gave them one last try.

The summer months are far less busy for me. The football season was over. I had only a little golf to attend to. Trying to take my mind off what was happening, I went up to Royal Lytham to report on the British Seniors' Open. I didn't tell anybody about the problem, basically hoping it would go away.

I was taking the drops every couple of hours. I had been warned that I might experience badly blurred vision. I remember that Gary Player was about to play the eighteenth hole. I wanted to see him into the clubhouse. I took the drops and left the press tent to walk across to the green. By the time I got there, I couldn't see three feet in front of me. I could hear the applause that greeted the South African's approach shot and his walk on to the putting surface but I couldn't see him. I felt so sorry for myself. I knew that if this carried on I wouldn't commentate on the Ryder Cup that was coming up in September. I'd never go to Anfield or Old Trafford or Highbury again. What would be the point? I couldn't work.

My next visit to the clinic was the decisive one. Mr Gupta had decided to operate on the right eye, the one that was giving him most concern. He had to choose one before the other. To operate on both at the same time was too big a risk and to do nothing would see me losing my sight.

The operation involves cutting into the eye to create an artificial channel through which fluid can escape, thereby relieving the pressure. Amazing really, I was only in hospital overnight. Before I left, Mr Gupta had declared the operation a success. Coincidentally, at the same time, the bombardment of drops had suddenly provoked a response in the left eye. The pressure dropped there too. The crisis was over.

I made that Ryder Cup. I still get to attend those football grounds that have become such a big part of my life. It's also part of my routine to see Mr Gupta or other members of his wonderful staff at Macclesfield Hospital every six months to check that the pressures around my eyes remain at acceptable levels. The complimentary letters I receive from blind listeners, for whom I am their eyes, are more important to me than any others. You understand why.

CHAPTER SIX

HEAVIES AND RED-TOPS

onsidering that any initial ambitions I had in a journalistic
career were in the world of newspapers, you'd think I'd share
an affinity with my colleagues in print. Unfortunately, though
I have many really good friends on that side of the business, I've
found as I've got older that I keep others at arm's length. There are
more than a few that I don't trust and some I wouldn't pass the time
of day with because of my lack of respect for them.

It wasn't always like this. When I first moved to England, I know I
benefited greatly from the advance preparations made for me by the
former sports editor of the *Belfast Telegraph*, Malcolm Brodie, who
used his considerable contacts to help ease the transition. He made
sure the likes of Peter Fitton and David Walker (the first now on the
Mail on Sunday, the latter a media director at Leeds United) looked
out for me. Peter and David remain close friends as well as colleagues.

But the agenda is different today. Broadcasters and writers are in
competition rather than in tandem. Let me explain. Say a newspaper
has a genuinely exclusive story. It remains exclusive only for as long

as it stays out of the public's hands. As soon as the first edition hits the streets, every other paper and media outlet can adopt the same story as its own. They may not have as much detail but they have enough to blur any 'exclusive' claim in the minds of the readers or the listeners.

Properly, any report of that story should be attributed to its original source. Too often, it isn't. It becomes: 'Newspaper reports say that so-and-so is leaving Manchester United and heading for Italy...' Frequently, the source is ignored altogether.

It works both ways. I once persuaded Graeme Souness to break his self-imposed silence some months after he'd resigned as manager of Liverpool. Graeme appeared on the Friday night chat programme which I presented on 5 Live at the time. It was heavily trailed and certain to attract attention from the papers. Sure enough, most northern editions led on the interview the following morning. Most didn't have the courtesy to mention the programme or, indeed, the BBC. The reporters just used the quotes. They might have been talking to Souness themselves except they knew and I knew that they hadn't.

I have to say that, most times, the arrangements are to the advantage of the broadcasters. There is little incentive for them to go hunting for stories when anything important is bound to fall in their laps anyway. Sad for the writers, but true. And that forces a different approach from the papers. What is the point of providing a straight-forward fact-by-fact account of a game when anyone who is interested has probably already watched it on television or heard it on radio? This is one of the main reasons why so much newspaper coverage is built around what the managers and players have to say rather than what the reporter thinks himself. It must frustrate the hell out of most of the writers. I know it would me.

This reliance on – and sensitivity about – quotes can be taken to ludicrous extremes. After any press conference, you see little huddles of reporters grouped together according to the audiences their papers appeal to – the dailies, the Sundays – broken down further into tabloids and heavies. What they're doing is deciding which comments to use and which line to take. Of course, individual reporters are able to do their own thing and it's my experience that the best do. But they're all under incredible pressure from their sports desks not to miss anything of importance.

I remember doing a League Cup tie, Huddersfield Town against Arsenal. The London side won comfortably, but I commented on Paul Merson's evident unhappiness when George Graham substituted him towards the end of the game. A few days later I bumped into Peter Fitton, who was then on the *Sun*. He told me, without malice, that I may have contributed to a colleague of his, Michael Morgan, getting the sack. Michael was the reporter at Leeds Road and when he'd filed his copy, his desk queried why he hadn't mentioned the row between Merson and Graham. 'What row?' said Michael. 'The one Alan Green talked about on the radio,' came the reply.

Michael scurried off to find out what he could. Not surprisingly, he met a brick wall. Denials all round. He told the desk, who insisted that he write about a row anyway. Michael refused. He wasn't going to write about something that I had seen but he hadn't. Quite right, too. But he did get into trouble and I guess, in a perverted way, I was somehow responsible. Thank God, he kept his job. To this day though, whenever we bump into each other at a match, he must dread it and spend the rest of the afternoon glued to the action in case he accidentally misses something that I talk about. I hope he's forgiven me. Michael's a good pro.

Increasingly, papers are paranoid about shielding whatever 'goodies' they have. In June 1999. I was in Sofia when England played Bulgaria in a European Championship qualifying match. I attended Kevin Keegan's press conference the day before the game. I rarely, if ever, go to managers' press conferences after matches. Too often, they're only interested in giving their version of events in the hope that it will kindly affect ours. I believe that the BBC pays me to give an honest report and interpretation of what I've seen. I've no wish to be influenced by others.

Anyway, I wanted to hear what Kevin had to say. Not with the slightest intention of reporting it but merely so that I would better understand for my commentary what might unfold the following evening. With England, radio interviews are conducted separately from the press. Therefore, Mike Ingham and a few others like Jonathan Pearce were waiting for Kevin in another room. I was the only broadcaster sitting with the newspaper reporters. I had no inkling of what was to happen.

Bluntly, I was asked to leave. Principally by the *Daily Telegraph*'s Henry Winter who, until that moment, I'd respected as a friend as well as one of our very best football writers. I asked him why. Henry said that the press conference was intended for the following day's newspapers and that, being present, I would be able to broadcast whatever Kevin said that night. I explained what I was doing there and that I hadn't the slightest intention of using anything in advance of this supposed embargo. I gave Henry, and the assembled gathering, my word on the matter. It seemed that wasn't enough. It was already a scene and I left before it deteriorated further. We had further words later, as I thought the *Daily Telegraph*'s football correspondent should be above considerations such as protecting quotes, and we haven't yet properly recovered our lost ground.

The stupid thing is that since the incident in Sofia, the Football Association has taken to printing quotations that arise from these press conferences. We may not be there but we get to read what's been said anyway. And there was something else that was forgotten that day. Namely, when we're all attending major tournaments, such as World Cups or European Championships, radio can sometimes have better access to managers and players or to more of them. There have been countless occasions when newspaper writers have had these interviews played back to them to help their work. Some appear to have forgotten that we need each other, and that we should really be cooperating.

I'm trying harder to be careful what I say and to whom I say it. I have learnt that, ridiculous though it is, such is the acreage of space allocated to sport in every newspaper that what broadcasters say and think, and how they behave, can often find its way into print. I was on a flight to Turin with Manchester United, on their way to play Juventus. It was a private charter and, as always, the group was split into two – directors and players up front, journalists safely separated from them at the rear. There's usually a fair amount of larking about. Generally, it's harmless, and it involves too many red wines and too many rude jokes. I've been as guilty as anyone, to my shame.

Des Kelly, now sports editor with the *Mirror*, was then football correspondent on the *Express*. Much laughter was being expended on me because of a particularly fierce haircut that I'd just had. Kelly seemed desperate to take a photograph. I later discovered why.

Getting back from Italy, I was told that my face figured in the *Express* and not in a flattering way. I bought a copy of the paper. Sure enough, there I was in big close-up; the photograph that Kelly had taken, against my wishes, on a private flight. Alongside it was a cartoon of a monk. Kelly wrote that he'd never understood why I had not been snapped up by television. Seeing my fat face and severe haircut, just like Friar Tuck, he understood better now. Perhaps he thought the column funny and of interest to the public. I didn't think it was either. I rang him at home. Unfortunately, I spoke only to his answering machine. I left a message asking why he'd done that. Was that the only thing a football correspondent could find to write about after two days in Turin watching Juventus and Manchester United?

The following morning, Kelly criticised me again in his column, because of my telephone message, saying that I took myself far too seriously.

Angry now, I rang Rob Shepherd, the *Express* sports editor. I asked him to justify what Kelly had done. I asked if he would like it if I, in retaliation, broadcast some of the things that go on during such trips. We both know that this is not always pretty. To his credit, Shepherd said he'd cool things down. I wish he would restrain the *Express*'s current sports gossip, Charlie Sale, who is forever trying to edge into the company of BBC people in the hope of catching some juicy tittle-tattle. This can easily lead to him misinterpreting what he has heard. It's like having enough knowledge to pass GCSE History but being wholly incapable of sitting a degree course. History is much more about understanding the significance and context of facts than reciting the facts themselves. So I am always wary of what I say when he is around in case it gives him what he mistakenly thinks is a story.

I have to accept that, for whatever reasons, I am a target for some newspapers. I'm outspoken, unafraid to say what I honestly believe, and occasionally that causes some controversy. 'Fergie and me' is a good example. Mostly because I care about some of the reporters who've found themselves at the wrong end of the United manager's wrath, I'll spare their blushes. But the *Daily Mail*, on one occasion, clearly didn't set out to spare my feelings. It came when I was having an awkward time at Old Trafford after I had had a public fall-out with Paddy Crerand, now resolved. Stirred up by some untrue articles written about me in fanzines I was again facing hostility from some supporters and so I was anxious for any bad feeling to subside. There should have been no reason for them to have anything against me, as I have nothing against the club or its fans.

Neil Wilson of the *Daily Mail* contacted me saying that the paper's sports editor was a big fan of mine and that they wanted to do an article about me. I had no reason to be fearful, as Wilson had a good reputation.

I met him at the Copthorne Hotel in Salford on the afternoon that Manchester United were playing Monaco in the European Cup. We talked for quite a while, about all the usual subjects. Then, as I expected, he started to talk about Alex. I explained that there were some areas I'd rather keep off the record, as I was trying to avoid making matters worse than they need be. He agreed, and after we'd covered the issue on the record, he switched his tape recorder off. I believed the rest would remain private.

The article appeared on the Saturday and I felt I'd been completely stitched up. Much that I thought was supposed to be private was printed. The headline, above my picture, ran: 'Why does this man [i.e. Fergie] hate me so much?' To be fair, there was nothing written that was untrue, and I had been accurately quoted. But it didn't help my situation with Manchester United. The paper was heavily entrenched in its own war with the United manager, involving the courts, and anything they could use to batter him with was fair game. I was merely a tool. In broadcasting they say 'Always assume the mike is live', and I had made the same mistake here with the newspaper.

I rang Neil Wilson at home, and on his mobile. Each time, I left my message, asking him to ring me, but he did not get back to me.

In general, relations with Old Trafford have improved, though I doubt that they will get on to a proper footing unless or until Ferguson leaves. I'm certainly glad that I agreed to do an interview this year for the *United We Stand* fanzine. It's edited by a guy called Andy Mitten, a United fanatic who, nevertheless, is intelligent enough to withstand criticism of the club and, if necessary, argue convincingly against it. Andy chatted to me about various issues that had come to represent AG v MU: 'Keane's a lout' and so on. Overwhelmingly, both magazine and I had a favourable response. The article went a long way to correcting some of the false impressions that had developed about me. However, a few days after the magazine appeared, Andy rang to tell me about the most incredible letter he'd received (anonymous, of course) slagging him off for not asking the right questions and suggesting others more appropriate, including the political situation in Northern Ireland. What on earth would that have to do with me, Manchester United and football? The very suggestion that I go round telephoning politicians to congratulate them on their latest achievements is ludicrous. But as with which football team I am supposed to support there are some people you will never convince about anything.

CHAPTER SEVEN

FRIENDS AND COLLEAGUES

BC Sport employs many people, yet I know very few of them well. The turnover in staff is vast and the penchant for short-term contracts is much in vogue. Particularly when I go to London on Fridays to host my programme, someone will say hello to me and I'll smile blankly in reply. I don't mean to be rude. It's simply that, most times, I don't recognise their faces, never mind know who they are. So please, if you're one of them, accept my apology.

But what of those that I do know? Look around your own workplace. Unless you're the boss, I'll guarantee that you'll be working with some people that you can't stand and, unfortunately, this is true for me as well.

Listeners assume, with the general air of bonhomie that surrounds commentary, that we're all the best of mates. That ain't necessarily so. I won't name names because, to a large degree, it's irrelevant. Once you're on air, personal differences must be swept aside. So if I can't bear to be in the company of X or, as is just as likely, he abhors being alongside me, you won't be able to tell.

I will say this. Mike Ingham and I really are good friends. Caj Sohal, one of the football producers, and another with whom I don't ever remember having a cross word, says the two of us go around like old women, tending to each other's needs. There are certain needs neither of us would attend to but, generally, Caj is right.

I spend almost as much time with Mike as I do with my wife. I know his moods. I know when he's angry, when he's concerned. I know when he needs to let off steam. You may find this hard to believe but even someone like me, who has so much to say for himself, can occasionally be a good listener. I also know when to back off and give him some time on his own. Mike likes to spend a few hours alone, particularly on the afternoon of a game abroad. Some producers like to believe that we're all boy scouts or girl guides and must do everything together – that we must all go to visit the Turin Shroud or, less ostentatiously, eat and drink as a group. I try to steer the guilty party away from such fanciful notions. Mike needs space and I, like a dutiful brother, try to ensure that he gets it.

I also believe that we like each other's company. After the World Cup final in 1998, BBC Radio Sport organised a big party. It wasn't our scene. Mike and I made our excuses, didn't attend and staged a private party of our own back at the hotel, accompanied only by a bottle of Chablis – or three!

We are, of course, very different in temperament and personality. If you compare our reports and our commentaries, you'll know that Mike is far less radical than I am. He is the correspondent and as a result, he takes his duties much more seriously than I do. Mike shoulders the responsibility of representing the BBC, whereas I represent only myself and my own views. If the bosses don't like what I say, no doubt they'll sack me.

I remember Mike being mortified on receiving a letter from some style policeman within the Corporation reminding him, and all the other correspondents, that they shouldn't offer opinions, merely balanced judgements. But what is football about if it's not about opinions? Mike, after due consideration, gave the missive the attention it deserved. He ignored it.

Of course, we love to tease each other, especially on air. At the start of the 1999–2000 season (i.e. the start of 'my' season – I always go on holiday during August, sensing, usually accurately, that nothing of significance ever happens before September), the first commentary I did was at Wembley. It was England's European Championship qualifier against Luxembourg. Mike started the game and spent much of the opening twenty minutes or so, in the company of his willing sidekick Terry Butcher, the former England captain, lambasting my absence throughout August. How good it was of me to show up again. How I only deigned to come out for the big games. That kind of thing. I reckoned they must have been missing me. They certainly kept on talking about me!

Now, if Mike is unduly sensitive about anything, it's about what he perceives to be an imbalance of goals described by the two of us. You must realise, all commentators have this paranoia. You believe that if you're working with a particular person, he'll get to describe many more goals than you will. I used to feel that way working with Ian Brown. Actually, I still do. But Mike will tell everyone who'll listen that he has this problem working with me.

At this point, I should inform you that of the three World Cup finals we've described together, I've yet to describe a single goal. Mike has commentated on all of them. Not that it hurts . . .

Anyway, I have to admit, Mike did have a strong case at the end of the previous season. I seemed to describe everything of significance, including that amazing goal from Ryan Giggs, in the tumultuous FA Cup semi-final replay between Manchester United and Arsenal at Villa Park. I was commentating when Andy Cole scored the title-clinching goal against Spurs. I described both Cup final goals and the two sensationally dramatic strikes in stoppage time in Barcelona. All the key moments in Manchester United's historic treble fell during my commentary spells and not in Mike's. No wonder he was still touchy about the topic come September.

I could sense his apprehension when he handed over commentary to me at Wembley. Despite the feeble nature of the opposition, England led only 1–0, and that goal had been a penalty. 'Now, to describe all the goals,' he said, 'here's Alan Green.' As if I'd do any such thing. There were only four more before half-time! Mike looked suicidal. I almost felt sorry for him. Terry and I were laughing so much we could barely commentate.

For Mike, the second half was even worse. There wasn't a goal in sight until, just before he was due to hand over for the second time, Stuart Pearce, who'd been recalled to the England team at the ripe old age of thirty-seven, appeared to have scored England's sixth goal. Mike gave it what we call, in commentary parlance, the 'full weigh-heigh'. He seized the moment and unleashed his frustrations in a marvellous description of the goal and its significance to the West Ham player. He passed the commentary to me with obvious satisfaction.

Unfortunately, the goal was disallowed for offside. I collapsed in laughter. Mike mimed removing the gun from its holster and pointed the barrel at his head, finger poised over the trigger.

From that point, with no wish to inflict further humiliation, I'd have been happy for the score to have remained at 5–0. However, Michael Owen came on as substitute and unleashed a ferocious shot in stoppage time. It was the headline goal of the match and duly led the highlights at the start of *Sports Report*. Mike could hardly bring himself to talk to me as he left the commentary position. Thankfully, the pain had eased by the time we boarded the flight to Warsaw on the following Monday and we resumed our normal relationship, having enormous fun together in an atmosphere of mutual respect.

You'll probably think it strange but I've never been to his house and he has never been to mine. I have only met his wife, Lorna, once and Mike's never met Brenda. There is no slight intended on either side. It's simply the way things are. It's probably healthy that we're able to divorce our private and working existences. Otherwise, I doubt our marriages would survive.

Mike is a great collector, of everything in general, but in particular, football programmes and records. If I'm at a game and he isn't, I try to remember to save him a programme. He's convinced that one day he'll bequeath his collection to his son, Marshall, who'll become a very wealthy man as a result. From what I know Marshall would exist very comfortably on Mike's accumulation of vinyl records.

I first became aware of this in 1990 when the two of us travelled to Moscow with England. I was amazed to discover that Mike had brought an empty suitcase with him. 'What for?' I asked. 'Records,' he said. He'd been told about this second-hand record store, some-where along one of the famous shopping areas of the city, the Arbat, and was determined to pay it a visit, bringing me along with him, of course. Mike scribbled the address that he'd been given on a piece of paper and proffered it to a decidedly dodgy Moscow cabbie. I dreaded the thought of where we might end up but, amazingly, he took us, at little expense, to this record store. I was mildly interested but not remotely as much as Mike. He was like a child let loose in a chocolate factory. Mike bought *one hundred and fifty* LPs! The case was barely adequate for the job. He acquired a dozen copies of the Beatles' *White Album* whose lyrics were written in Cyrillic. He gave me one as a thank you and I still have it, tucked away somewhere. Mike is convinced – and who am I to doubt him

– that they'll all be worth a fortune one day.

A year later, the *Daily Mirror*'s Harry Harris and I found ourselves standing alongside Mike in a dubious second-hand record shop in Detroit, Michigan. We were in the States covering the US Cup, meant as England's warm-up for the World Cup itself in 1994 (Graham Taylor's team didn't make it).

Mike was in his element. There were untold vinyl riches at his fingertips. He didn't know where to start. After two hours, Harry and I decided that boredom had got the better of us and we left him to get on with it. I feel guilty to this day. We had forgotten what a dangerous city Detroit is and we'd left a colleague alone in one of its worst areas. Mike . . . sorry, it will never happen again!

I love the guy. I'm very privileged to work with him and I hope the BBC appreciates how lucky it is that the two main men in radio get on so well. It wasn't always thus.

Our predecessors were Peter Jones and Bryon Butler. Everyone knew that, however much mutual respect there was, they weren't that close. Peter once told me how they had done a game together at St James' Park, Newcastle. They'd shared a train on the way up from London and Peter was determined there would be no such arrangement on the way back. He made some spurious excuse to leave Bryon at the ground and hurried to the station intent on catching an earlier train than they'd intended. Peter made it with a couple of minutes to spare and settled into his first class seat, whisky in hand, looking forward to the journey ahead. Suddenly, he glimpsed Bryon scurrying along the platform and, to the amusement of his fellow passengers, Peter fell to the floor hoping Bryon would avoid seeing him. Bryon got into a different carriage and probably didn't know until this day that he was on the same train as Peter.

For what it's worth, I adored both of them. Jonesy was the doyen of football commentary. We all looked up to him and he remains the only person who has ever given me advice on the art. Typically, it was simple but incisive. 'Light and shade, Alan, always offer a contrast. Paint pictures. Use your voice to emphasise what's important and what isn't.'

Peter taught me some of the ways to hold an audience, even if the game is poor or the outcome long decided. I will never forget listening to a match he did with Eddie Hemmings, now Sky Sports' excellent rugby league presenter and commentator. 'So,' said Eddie, 'at the midway point of the second half here at Anfield, in this FA Cup replay, it's Liverpool 6 York City 1. Over to Peter Jones.' Now that scenario is a nightmare for any commentator. The game was over. It was inconceivable that York could have made a contest of it. Yet Jonesy still made it sing. He held our interest. He found things away from the game to talk about. I didn't even think of switching off.

No one 'painted the picture' better than he did. As a former headmaster, he was accustomed to making the best possible use of the English language. His eloquence at the microphone was, and remains, unmatched. Yet as I have mentioned he did invent the odd picture as well.

Bryon was a supreme wordsmith. Give him time, and the right subject, and BB would deliver a better voice-piece than anyone else. A week after the Hillsborough tragedy, driving home from Bramall Lane, I had to stop the car. Bryon's report from an empty Anfield had me crying helplessly. It was a magnificent rendition, enriched by Bryon's fabulously deep voice. I remember it still.

Yet, and he'll admit it himself, he wasn't the best of commentators. Bryon cared too much for the value of vocabulary to deliver words as quickly, and sometimes thoughtlessly, as many commentators do. Instead, he liked to script the odd paragraph of prose and drop it into his commentary, as seamlessly as possible of course. Sometimes it didn't work.

One day, at Selhurst Park, he was commentating on Crystal Palace and Swansea City playing in the FA Cup. Bryon, reading from a prepared note, had momentarily taken his eyes off the game. The roar of the crowd signified that it was time to look up again. He saw that the ball was in the net. Breaking off from his wholesome description of somebody's family background, or previous footballing record, Bryon declared: 'Yo! It's there! It's there! And that's the goal that could take Swansea City into the next round of the FA Cup. And such was the quality of that goal [which he hadn't seen], the Crystal Palace fans are on their feet applauding. It's Crystal Palace 1 Swansea City 3.'

To his massive credit, when he made the occasional gaffe, Bryon was usually quick to acknowledge it. As on this occasion. 'Hold it. Hold it,' he said. 'Egg on face. It's Crystal Palace 2 Swansea City 2!' Bryon had the wrong team scoring the goal!

Because they happened so rarely, Bryon's gaffes became classics. In 1980, he was commentating in Barcelona as England played Spain. Now the Spanish had a famous cheerleader called Manolo who used to wander around the stadium, wherever Spain were playing, beating a huge drum, whipping up support. In the pre-match production meeting, John Helm, who was in charge of the outside broadcast, told the two commentators, Bryon and Peter Jones: 'Don't forget to mention Manolo. At some stage, he's bound to be banging that drum right in front of you. Do remember to tell the listeners what's going on.'

Manolo performed as usual. Bryon was commentating at the time and the Spanish rabble-rouser was almost sitting in his lap. Unfortunately, Bryon appeared oblivious to the situation. John glanced at him. Still Bryon ignored Manolo. So Helm resorted to the standard production play. He wrote a note – 'Mention the drummer' – and passed it in front of Bryon.

'So,' says Bryon, 'England have a corner. It's from the right. Cunningham to take it. There it goes [he glances down], mention the drummer, headed away from the near post.'

To this day, Bryon refuses to acknowledge that he said any such thing, but we all know the truth. Some of us even have the commentary on tape!

The 'Cunningham' was Laurie Cunningham. He'd just been transferred from West Bromwich Albion to Real Madrid. He'd only been on the pitch a few minutes, coming on as substitute for Tony Woodcock. Bryon said: 'And on comes Cunningham of Real Madrid and now of Spain!' On this occasion, it was Peter Jones who passed the note. 'ENGLAND substitute,' it reminded Bryon, to which BB responded: 'And England are going to make a substitution as well!'

But my favourite Bryon story is one I was involved in. We'd gone with England to Tbilisi to watch them play the Soviet Union in a warm-up game for the 1986 World Cup. The stadium was awful and the commentary position was worse, far too far from the halfway line and behind a glass screen that hadn't been cleaned in a very long time. The Russians wore the old Adidas shirts. All the numbers were made up of three lines and, from our restricted view, it was going to prove very difficult to distinguish the 8 from the 3, or the 9 from the 6, and so on.

Bryon started the game and immediately I was struck by how fluent he was. 'Kosygin to Brezhnev. Now Tolstoy to Korsakov. And to Krushchev on the wing . . .' Hold on a second, I thought, that's not Krushchev – Krushchev's the goalie. He isn't playing right midfield! I looked across. Bryon had written a list of the Russian names on a piece of paper and stuck it with Sellotape on to the window. He wasn't even trying to identify the Russians. He seemed to me merely to be calling their names out by rota. The listeners probably never noticed!

Truth be told, I got the feeling that Bryon clearly never rated me. I don't know if it was my particular style that he disliked, or simply me as a person, but I often thought he'd rather I wasn't around. Perhaps it goes back to that day at Tottenham when we were commentating together. And I was told to finish the game.

He certainly made his feelings obvious to me a year or two back when I was sitting waiting to commentate on Aston Villa versus Liverpool. I felt a tap on my shoulder and turned to see Bryon in the row behind: 'Hi BB, how are you?'

'Fine,' said Bryon, 'just remember, dear boy, there's no need to shout.' I'm sorry, but no matter how fine a correspondent Bryon Butler was, a very fine one, we should accept the styles we each adopt – and I feel very comfortable with my approach.

Some of the best young commentary talent to emerge from BBC Radio in recent years, like Rob Hawthorne and Jon Champion, never got to do an FA Cup final or an England international. Mike Ingham and Alan Green were always there in front of them. It must have been frustrating and they each moved on, to television. I'm delighted both succeeded so well there. They're great guys.

I sometimes get the feeling that one or two of the current bunch, behind us in the queue, are finding it difficult to rein in their frustrations. Such is the expansion of commentary under 5 Live Sport, everyone these days gets to do European ties and internationals, but only Mike and I continue to be there on the really big occasions. It's too easily forgotten that we waited behind Jonesy and BB for many years and I don't recall either of us bitching about the situation when, believe me, we had far fewer crumbs of comfort. I am sure their day will come. But, I hope, not too soon.

CHAPTER EIGHT

SIDEKICKS

Just as I was beginning to find my feet as a commentator, in the early eighties, the former Head of Radio Sport, Pat Ewing, someone who liked me as much as I liked her (sic), did her level best to deflate me. She suggested I needed voice training. She might have added that sticking a couple of golf balls in my mouth might achieve the desired effect; that is, diminish the accent and produce the typical middle-England drawl that was still largely prevalent in the BBC at the time.

More significantly, during the same interview, she told me: 'You've far too much to say for yourself. You're saying the kind of things that should be left for summarisers to say. You're straying into their territory.'

In this at least, she was partly right. However, as usual, she missed the main point. Somewhat less than diplomatically, I responded: 'Give me a summariser with something to say and I'll happily let them get on with it.' The truth is that too many of the summarisers then had little or nothing of consequence to say, justifying their presence at the microphone merely because of who they were, who they'd played for, how many caps they'd won or who they'd managed.

Today, it's rather different and I like to believe I've played at least a small part in forcing summarisers to 'come out', to be more forthright. I have always been highly opinionated and I am not very sympathetic to those of wimpish views. So if a summariser tries to sit on the fence, I'll do my best to push him off it. Partly as a consequence, those I work with these days are much less inclined to make the diplomatic comment and are far more ready to say what they actually think, just as they would if they were sitting in a pub talking to their mates.

I'm asked frequently who I like working with most. It's not a cop-out when I say that I like almost all of them, and usually for different reasons. The perfect summariser has achieved a lot in the game, domestically and internationally, as a player and as a manager. He understands it. He has a good, strong voice. He is current but isn't burdened by being too close to those he's making comments about. He has opinions and isn't afraid to voice them. He has an acute sense of humour and of occasion. In a roundabout way, what I'm telling you is that the perfect summariser doesn't exist. They all have weaknesses as well as strengths.

I used to work with Denis Law. No former player, in my experience, is more beloved by fans than Denis. Wherever he goes, he's besieged by autograph hunters, no matter whether they support Manchester United or not. Affection for the Scot seems to transcend any tribal loyalties. People admire him for having been a fantastic player and for still being a thoroughly nice man. And, obviously, he was a natural choice as a summariser once his playing days ended.

Denis was wonderful at reflecting the emotions of an important match. He conveyed his feelings beautifully. He loves the game with a passion. Yet I learnt quickly not to ask him why something had happened. It soon became clear to me that he'd been such an instinctive player he never thought to ask himself about it. Denis didn't analyse the reason, for taking up a certain position; he just 'knew'. How, therefore, could he explain why someone else did something the way they did or why a move broke down or why it succeeded?

I love Denis. I haven't seen him in a long time, which I greatly regret. His disappearance from BBC Radio had nothing to do with the commentators. Someone in the hierarchy decided Denis didn't quite fit in any more. Either that or Denis himself got fed up dealing with the frequent frustrations of working for the BBC. Either way, I'd like to believe that he still considers me a friend. He certainly once did.

You see, you knew you'd been accepted into Denis's inner circle when he asked you to go to the toilet with him. I'd better explain. Though Denis never complained about the attention he got, he always appreciated a certain amount of chaperoning when he was in the vicinity of the general public, particularly when he was going to the loo. I nearly fainted the first time he asked me to accompany him but he told me the reason why, and after that, I treated such requests as testament to how well we got on. I should emphasise that Denis is a great family man!

Like many current and former footballers, Denis likes to have the occasional drink and he has a technique he employs if he is having a drink in public, say in the lounge bar of a hotel. Denis always sits in a chair that is facing a corner. He's less likely to be recognised that way. Mind you, in my time, he also used the excuse of public attention as a reason not to go to the bar to buy a round of drinks. I swear that Denis carried the same £10 note in his wallet for years!

Jimmy Armfield is of the same generation as Denis. Another star who played the game when you didn't make a fortune. In BBC terms, he's long outlasted the Scot. Jim was already a top-rank summariser long before I came on to the scene and I've no doubts he'll still be around when I've gone. I once broached the subject of his retirement with his wife, Ann. 'No,' she said, 'Jim will never give it up. It's in his blood. I can't think what he'd do if he ever stopped talking about football.'

Jim's done it all. He was one of the greatest players Blackpool ever produced and displayed a loyalty to the club that's rare to find nowadays. Jim only ever played for Blackpool. Spurs once made a serious move for him, offering him huge money to move to London, but he never even got round to talking to them. Blackpool bought him a house to help persuade him to stay and Jim's lived in that house ever since. He's that sort of guy.

He played for and captained England and was unfortunate to be edged out of Sir Alf Ramsey's starting line-up in the 1966 World Cup. But, in the joyous scenes that followed England's 4–2 extra-time victory over West Germany, I remember vividly the contrast between the expression on the face of Jimmy Greaves, who found it so hard to accept his non-selection, and that of Jim whose beaming smile suggested he'd actually been among those out there playing, though he hadn't. Jim harbours no bitterness towards anybody.

Not even to the Leeds players who used to chide him about his legendary slowness in making up his mind. The late Billy Bremner once told me how Jim, then manager at Elland Road, used to suck long and hard on his pipe before answering a question or delivering a decision: 'His indecision was final.' Those players still respected him enormously and he rewarded them by doing something Don Revie never achieved, taking Leeds to the European Cup final in 1975 in Paris where they were robbed of victory against Bayern Munich by some highly contentious refereeing.

When I consider the various contributions that Jim has made to football outside of playing and managing, his role at the Football Association in which he was instrumental in the choice of two England managers, his current job in the coaching department of the

Professional Footballers' Association, his media work for the BBC and formerly the *Daily Express*, I find it astounding that he was never recognised in the honours lists until the summer of 2000 when he finally received an OBE. Indeed, given the way certain football knighthoods, OBEs and MBEs have been thrown around – Ian Wright springs readily to mind – it's nothing short of disgraceful that Jimmy Armfield has been ignored. He wouldn't admit it but I know it must have meant a great deal to him when it finally happened.

I always feel as if Jim treats me like a son. He knows that my outspoken manner frequently takes me close to the edge of trouble so, every now and again, there's a comforting arm around the shoulder and a soft word of advice, an inquiry about my health or workload or my family. I may not always make it obvious but I greatly appreciate his friendship.

Jim and I spent a lot of time together during the 1994 World Cup in the United States, when we spearheaded the main team on the west coast, in Los Angeles and San Francisco. Jim was in the car with me as I drove along the twelve-lane freeway from the airport towards downtown LA. We'd flown in separately and met by the baggage carousel . . . eventually. Jim had gone to the wrong one! He was still smoking a pipe then and had the air of a man who'd seen and done it all before, whereas I was more than a little nervous arriving in the 'City of Angels' for the first time in my life. It was agreed that I would drive, and Jim would direct me to our hotel by reading the map. Some hope.

Within minutes we were lost. There must be thirty Holiday Inns in Los Angeles and we hadn't a clue how to find the one we'd been booked into. After a couple of hours, I was getting quite worried and more than a little angry. Luckily, we eventually stumbled across a Holiday Inn and wandered into the lobby hoping that it was the right one. 'No, Sir,' said the man on reception, 'the one you are looking for is south-side of downtown. I can direct you but are you really sure that you want to stay there?' Now I really had cause to worry. He told us that the location was in South Central LA – gangland. I rang the BBC World Cup headquarters in Dallas. I hadn't even seen the hotel but I knew it wasn't the sort of place that I wanted to stay in for the next seventeen days. They were going to have to find somewhere else, anywhere else.

Reluctantly, I drove to the allocated hotel. It was worse than I could have imagined. The only signs of life in the vicinity were the gang ribbons that adorned the street lamps, indicating which mob controlled the area, and the liquor store at the corner of the block outside of which a drunk was lying asleep on the sidewalk. I still see the hotel on my fairly frequent visits back to the city. You can spot it from Interstate 10 as you speed through Los Angeles. Seeing it from the freeway is as close as I intend to get.

I rang Dallas again. 'This place is entirely unacceptable. We want out.' It was explained to me that a different, hopefully more attractive, hotel had been found in Santa Monica but that it wasn't available until the next day and, unfortunately, we had to stay in the Holiday Inn for one night. Jim and I held a pow-wow. Neither of us liked the situation but there was no way of avoiding it. I suggested that we drive out to Santa Monica to check out the proposed hotel. At the very least, it would get us away from this place for a few hours.

Clearly, the BBC knew they'd been in the wrong and wanted to make amends. The Loews Hotel in Santa Monica was everything we could have wished for. It was superbly located with direct access to the beach and the Pacific Ocean. Our boat had definitely come in, though I was careful not to let the BBC know how pleased we were. I had won the mind game. Later, when we stayed overnight on a trip up to San Francisco, a bottle of chilled champagne was delivered to each of our rooms as an apology.

Before that, though, we had no option but to survive the night in South Central LA. I shut every bolt on my room door, of which there were six! Sleep didn't seem a viable option but, somehow, I nodded off, bolstered by jet-lag and the exhausting travel that day.

A shattering noise woke me up. Despite the blackout blinds that covered the bedroom window, I could see flashing lights. Outside, there was a voice screaming: 'GET AWAY FROM THIS CAR! YOU'RE TOO CLOSE TO THE CAR! I WARN YOU! GET AWAY FROM THE CAR!' God . . . it had to be the police apprehending a gangster! It's my first night in LA and there's going to be a shoot-out outside my hotel!

Sometimes, I'm stupid as well as inquisitive. I got out of bed and edged back the curtains. I couldn't miss whatever might happen. Reality quickly struck me. It was nothing but a bloody car alarm! One of those idiotic voice response ones designed to frighten the life out of anyone who sets it off, accidentally or otherwise. It certainly frightened me. Further sleep was now totally out of the question. It was with the greatest relief imaginable that Jim and I set off the next morning for the opulence of Santa Monica, though I made just one further mistake. I let Jim talk the Loews into giving him the room next to mine.

Considering the contribution that Jim makes to football, at so many different levels, he can be, as Bobby Robson once said of Paul Gascoigne, 'as daft as a brush'. It's impossible not to like Jim but occasionally he does act as if he's not all there. During that World Cup, he'd also stayed at another Loews Hotel, a massive complex in Dallas which had several lobbies and innumerable restaurants. You can imagine the vast turnover in guests at a place like that. Jim was sitting having dinner in one of the restaurants as part of a large BBC group. Everyone had ordered except for Jim. He was still studying the menu intensely. The waiter was getting impatient, so were the other diners. 'Oh,' said Jim, handing the menu back, 'I'll just have what I had last night!' As if the waiter knew him from Adam and knew what he wanted.

Anyway, early one morning in Santa Monica, there was a knock on my door. It was Jim. 'I've lost my Visa card,' he said. 'It was in my wallet in the hotel safe and it's not there any more.'

'What? The wallet's gone?'

'No, just the credit card.'

'That's odd. They took a credit card but not the wallet. And from the hotel safe? Hang on Jim, I thought you once told me that you'd never have a credit card?'

'Well, I don't. It's not really mine. It came in the post before the World Cup. I just stuck it in my wallet. It must have been the BBC that sent it to me. I'll ring them in Dallas.'

'No, no, no, don't do that, Jim. The BBC doesn't send out credit cards. You've got to ring Visa. By the way, you did sign this card before you put it in your wallet?'

'No, it's not mine. It has my name on it but it's not mine.'

'Jim, have I got this right? You had a credit card, in your name, but you haven't signed it and it's been lost or stolen?'

'Yes.'

'Get on the phone to Visa this second and explain what's happened. If that card's been stolen, someone will have just written your name in and they'll be out somewhere spending a fortune. Ring Visa now!'

A few minutes later, there was another knock on the door. Jim. 'I rang Dallas and they say it hasn't anything to do with the BBC. They didn't send the card.'

'Jim, I *told* you that. Don't waste any more time. RING VISA!'

Another delay. Then the door was knocked again. 'I've rung Visa. They say they've got no record of my card. They've told me to ring my bank.'

I looked at my watch to check the time difference. 'You've just got time, Jim. The bank won't be shut yet. Ring them. It doesn't matter what it costs. This is too important.'

The final knock on the door. 'I've rung the bank and they've checked everything. They tell me they're certain that I haven't got a credit card. For certain.'

'What's this all about then?'

'Well, I've been thinking. I reckon it was only an application form for a credit card that was in the wallet. I really don't have a card at all.'

'Jim, you know, if I was your bank manager, I'd put a big black dot alongside your name. Not only would I never give you a credit card, I wouldn't let you have a cheque book!' Typically, Jim just laughed and left.

He really was great fun to be with on that trip. He's such an enthusiast for the game. I remember driving away from the Rose Bowl after the final. Mike Ingham and I were very quiet. We didn't need to say to one another what we were thinking. We were both acutely depressed by the quality of the game. All the anticipation before the tournament began. All the hard work and effort and fun of traipsing across America for nearly six weeks. And it had to finish with an absolute stinker! But Jim? He was whistling and singing in the car. No matter the disappointment of the game, he was still thrilled at being there. Perhaps Mike and I were wrong. I suspect that we'll both lose our love for football long before Jim does.

Or Terry Butcher. Way before I first met 'Butch', those pictures of that bloodstained forehead in Stockholm told me this was someone you wanted to have on your side – in every sense. The former England captain, who's been our main international summariser since 1996, is a great team player. There isn't anyone more prepared to muck in than he is and we've had some great times together, particularly during France 98.

Mike Ingham, as correspondent, needed to stay the whole time with England at their headquarters in La Baule. Apart from commentating on England's matches, Mike had to do all the other reports and interviews surrounding the activities of the national team. It would have been wildly extravagant for Terry and I, the other members of the 'England team', to have based ourselves alongside Mike. Quite properly, we were charged with chasing round France commentating on other matches. We had a ball.

I first met up with Terry in Marseille. I had been in Paris for the opening game and the next day flew down to the south coast. Butch had earlier flown in from Edinburgh. For a time, he'd run a hotel and restaurant near the Scottish capital and he still lives in the area. Though I'd never been there, I'm assured it was of the highest standards. To say the least, our accommodation in Marseille was somewhat short of those standards. It was a dump. Now I know you'll be wondering what I'm complaining about; I was lucky to be there. And I was. But you'll have gathered by now that we don't always stay in the lap of luxury and this truly was a very poor hotel. More like a motel – a run-down motel.

Butch didn't complain; he rarely does. Immediately, he set about making the best of what we had. Organising al-fresco lunches of fresh baguettes, cheese, tomatoes and, of course, some select wines. Outside of the games, it was like being on holiday. Until England arrived for the match against Tunisia: not so much England but the England fans.

We knew there'd be trouble. It's partly because so many of 'our boys' go looking for trouble. Their whole demeanour, even the way they dress, helps provoke it. But I have to say that on this occasion the locals, that is the North African immigrant population in Marseille, were equally game. Few of the French that I spoke to in the days after the rioting laid the blame solely at the feet of the English. They could see it coming too. The shame was that there wasn't a hint of bother in any of the other matches that Terry and I did in Marseille. In the circumstances, you couldn't help but be embarrassed by what our mob had done.

Mind you, who am I to be talking about the combined dangers of sun and alcohol? I lost a day of my life in Marseille! In the nicest possible way . . .

We had a day off. Ron Jones had joined us temporarily, the three of us due to work together on Holland against South Korea the following evening. Nobody wanted to cramp each other's style so we decided to go our separate ways, agreeing that we would probably meet up for dinner later in the day. I fancied I'd take a book down to the beach which was only a few hundred yards from the hotel, across a very busy road and through an area of park land. Making my way there, I thought I'd give Mike a ring in La Baule to make sure he was working as hard as he was supposed to be. I'd just made contact when I practically tripped over Terry, who was also heading for the beach. The two of us continued on our way, chatting to Mike on the mobile as we went.

As we arrived near the shore, a very attractive woman jumped up from where she'd been sunbathing and shouted and waved in our direction. She was wearing sunglasses and I genuinely didn't recognise Alex Dalton, one of the producers in the department, who was on holiday in the region. Mischievously, I teased Mike that I had to go because I was about to be propositioned by a beautiful girl! We all had a laugh at his expense and sat down in the sunshine. It was a glorious day. It wasn't any later than ten in the morning but the temperature was already in the 80s.

Nearing lunchtime, somebody, probably me, suggested we find

somewhere to go and have a beer. No one needed encouragement. It really sounded a good idea at the time. We found a little pizza place by the roadside and sat down thinking: 'Ain't this the life!' Terry, whose eyesight is much better than mine, spotted Ron crossing the road and chased after him. On reflection, another bad idea. Now there were four possible rounds of drinks rather than three. In truth, I don't know how many rounds of drinks we went through. We were certainly popular with our restaurant hosts, who kept bringing us free pizzas.

It must have been five o'clock when I decided it was time to return to my room to sleep off whatever damage had been done. I was in something of a bad way, but it was to get worse. For all of us.

The phone rang. It was Alex. Was I ready for dinner? What dinner!? She said we had arranged to go out for a meal. I was so disorientated I didn't know whether 'we' meant four or two. Had I asked Alex out? A married man with two kids? What mess was I in?

Alex came to the door. She was obviously dressed ready for dinner whereas I was fit only to resume my sleep. Sheepishly, disgracefully, I explained that I really couldn't go out in this state. Not unreasonably, she left in a state of mild temper. What I didn't know then was that it really was meant to be a 'four' and that Alex hadn't been able to make any contact with the other two. They were even worse than me!

What had happened was this. When I left the pizza restaurant, both Ron and Terry noticed that an impromptu game of football was taking place in the park area near the beach. They fancied joining in but the locals turned them away. Imagine, a man who'd captained his country couldn't even get himself picked for a game of beach football. Butch was furious and stormed off towards the supermarket to buy himself a baguette. He could see the supermarket no more than seventy-five yards away. Getting there was something else. No matter how he tried, the supermarket never seemed to be any closer. Terry was seriously tipsy. Indeed, the only knowledge he had of what followed was finding a till receipt from the supermarket in his trouser pocket the next morning! Lost in Marseille.

Ron was worse still. He can be stubborn, our Ron. He wouldn't give up on trying to get a game. He hung around and waited for the next one to begin. Sure enough, this time he was selected but as soon as the match started, he began to sense that this wasn't the brightest thing he'd done in his life. He was wobbling all over the place. Suddenly, he saw the ball come floating in the air towards him. Every instinct he had, except for common sense, told him to head it. Ron headed it. It felt as if his head had exploded. He collapsed on the ground. The game continued around him, yet he knew he couldn't get to his feet. He had no option but to crawl on his hands and knees to the side of the pitch. He thought, I'll just close my eyes and have a rest. Then I'll feel better. Another mistake.

Ron woke up. It was now dark. The game had finished and he'd been sleeping rough in one of the most dangerous cities in the world. Got to get back to the hotel, but how? There was a six-lane road to cross, populated by drivers whose sole *raison d'être* seemed to be to knock down as many pedestrians as possible. Ron knew there was a pedestrian crossing but in his less than entirely sober state, he couldn't figure out how it worked. Every time he shaped to cross, another car flew straight in front of him. He had no option. He waited fully half an hour until someone else – it happened to be 'an old woman' – helped him across the road.

All three of us were a mess the next morning. In every tournament, believe me, there's always at least one day like that when everyone goes completely off the rails. Trouble was, we had to commentate on South Korea that night. Heaven knows how, but I can honestly say it was one of the best commentaries of the World Cup. Ron was simply brilliant: not one misidentification, not one mispronunciation. It was a miracle.

Mark Lawrenson worked for BBC Television during that World Cup, staying in a plush hotel in Paris. I'm sure he wouldn't have had it any other way but his company was badly missed on the road, which is where he usually is for BBC Radio.

With Lawro, you can be absolutely certain of having a good time, on and off the air. He's truly an expert in that area. He is also probably the only summariser with whom I'm careful about getting into any verbal sparring. Mark is fearless. If, occasionally, he goes a little too far and then suddenly realises it, his trademark response is a shrug of the shoulders, an impish grin and a loud chuckle.

Because of what he achieved as a player, because of the respect that he commands, Mark's inclination to be highly critical is generally accepted by his peers. It's the same with Alan Hansen. They know: they should be listened to.

Mark hardly ever gets it wrong and as a result, I pay attention when he says something. Newcastle were playing a Champions League game against Barcelona in the Nou Camp. It should have been a great occasion but, the outcome being fairly meaningless, it wasn't. It was a dull game and it was proving quite difficult to maintain our concentration. That's an excuse that I'm getting in early here. The other was that we were in our customary wretched commentary position there. Stuck over a corner flag, so high we could touch a passing cloud.

Newcastle were making a substitution. Mark, who had been for a time the defensive coach at St James' Park, mused on the wisdom or otherwise of bringing on Stuart Elliott, a young, untried defender. I never thought to check.

It must have been a quarter of an hour before I heard the first

The media attention given to football has never been greater, as can clearly be seen in this photo taken during Euro 2000. But we must question if the demands of television are healthy for the game. (*Ben Radford/Allsport*)

In this new age few have benefited as much as David Beckham, whose every new haircut is carefully scrutinised – even by my daughter. (*Alex Livesey/Allsport*)

With United 3–2 up at Anfield in September 1999, Fergie makes sure he reminds the referee that time is up. (*Ross Kinnaird/Allsport*)

On a bus in Moscow with Manchester United in 1992. These were the days when Fergie and I hadn't completely stopped talking. (*Empics*)

Some of my most terrifying experiences commentating have been in Turkey as when Manchester United were welcomed to hell by Galatasaray fans in 1993.
(*Clive Brunskill/Allsport*)

The only time I've ever smiled in Turkey, during a trip with England to Izmir.

During my early days as a commentator: here I am just behind Bob Paisley as he receives the League Cup in 1983. (*Daily Star*)

Emile Heskey and Fabrizio Ravanelli watch the ball with mild interest during the 1997 League Cup final, one of the most tedious games I've ever watched. (*Colorsport*)

telling chuckle coming from Mark's direction. Elliott had just won another crunching challenge and played the ball securely left-footed up the field. Mark had previously wondered why such a right-footed player had been positioned on the left side of Newcastle's defence. Now, he had caught on but I still hadn't.

'You know Elliott, the substitute who came on a while back?' He continued: 'Well . . . it isn't him at all. That's Stuart Pearce!'

I didn't know whether to laugh or cry. We had both managed to misidentify someone who's played in a World Cup semi-final, won nearly eighty caps and captained his country! There was no point trying to cover it up. We laughingly held our hands up in shame at making such a mistake. Funny thing was, the other commentator, who shall remain nameless, maintained he knew all along that we'd got it wrong. I wonder why he didn't tell us.

Mark and I flew back to Manchester the following morning on Air France via Paris. Our plane took off late from Barcelona and lost further time during the flight. When we landed at Charles de Gaulle, it seemed there were only minutes remaining before we were due to step on to the connecting flight. I couldn't see how we'd make it, particularly when, as is the habit at that airport, the plane hadn't parked at a gate. We had to catch a bus to reach Terminal D and the plane for Manchester departed from Terminal B.

Worse, the bus was caught in traffic. My panic was increasing, though typically Mark just kept on saying we'd be fine. I made sure that I was first to jump off the coach when it reached the terminal building and ran through the door. What relief! There was an Air France stewardess holding up a sign: MANCHESTER. Terrific, I thought, they've really got their act together.

There were five of us in all. She said we'd have to hurry. We ran up the stairs, through the gate, across Terminal D, out the main entrance, into Terminal B, across the concourse, through the now abandoned gate, down the stairs and . . . on to another bus!

The traffic was just as bad but I knew now that there was no chance of the plane taking off without us. For the first time in about thirty frantic minutes, I started to relax. I even felt pleased about the likelihood that I'd shed some weight. I'd sweated buckets.

However, my mood changed as we drew up to the plane. There was something familiar about it. But no, it couldn't be. Air France couldn't be that incompetent. Oh, but they were! I called the cabin stewardess over. 'Can you tell me, has this plane just flown in from somewhere else?'

'Yes.'

'Where from?'

'Barcelona.'

You couldn't make it up. Lawro collapsed.

Now, you mustn't get the impression that I get on with all the summarisers. I don't. One or two of them have got right up my nose. Martin Chivers, particularly. The former Spurs and England striker used to be a regular on the circuit. I'd never had a problem with him, though I was inclined to think he was something of a show-off.

I was at White Hart Lane for a UEFA Cup tie against Rapid Vienna. Spurs were trailing after the first leg. I sat with Martin in the directors' guest lounge discussing what we thought might happen during the evening. We both agreed the last thing Tottenham needed to do was to go frantically on the attack. Best to be patient, confident that the breakthrough would come.

Martin and I went to the commentary position to do a report for the main sports desk before the start of the game. I'd told him what I was going to say. '. . . so, Martin, the last thing Spurs should do is adopt the gung-ho approach.'

'Couldn't disagree more, Alan, Tottenham have to go at the

Austrians right from the off!' And he continued in similar vein. I couldn't believe it. If he genuinely disagreed with me, that was fine, but that wasn't what he was saying beforehand. I felt he was being too clever by half.

The match commentary confirmed my opinion. He had definitely decided to contradict everything I said. Even in factual matters. If I called a corner, he'd say it was a throw-in. My 'free-kick to Vienna' was his 'should have gone to Spurs'. I even tested my theory by deliberately saying something I knew to be wrong and, yes, this time he called it right. It was perverse and I didn't understand. After that, I told the football producer that I'd never work with Martin Chivers again, and I haven't.

CHAPTER NINE

HILLSBOROUGH AND BEYOND

I was so looking forward to the game, to the occasion. Then, FA Cup semi-finals were still played alongside one another on a Saturday afternoon. There was always a special gravitas about the announcement on the following *Sports Report*: 'The FA Cup final in May will be between X and Y. . . .' Wonderful. Rather like the way everyone used to love hearing the draw for the various rounds unfold via radio and Lancaster Gate on Monday lunchtimes. Between the two of them, television and the Football Association need no help in tearing down the institutions of the game we love.

I remember this particular semi-final afternoon, 15 April 1989, as being especially beautiful. I parked my car in Hillsborough Park, barely five minutes' walk from the stadium. I was glad that I'd chosen to wear a short-sleeved shirt. I was already beginning to sweat in the sunshine before I reached the relieving shadow of the main entrance. Though the players may have regretted that early summer warmth, it seemed the perfect weather for watching football. Particularly watching two of the finest teams in the country, Liverpool and Nottingham Forest.

I'd also commentated on the meeting between the pair in the previous year's semi-final, won by Liverpool, and also at Hillsborough. I don't remember much of that game. My memories of the final itself are much more vivid. Wimbledon, ugly Wimbledon, the 'anti-football' team, led 1–0 but Liverpool were awarded a penalty. I was commentating. I swear I hadn't prepared for such a moment, though in those days, I did far more preparation for games, especially big games. I knew that John Aldridge had never missed a penalty and that no penalty had ever been missed in an FA Cup final at Wembley. The odds were stacked against Dave Beasant. So, with suitable build-up, I remember being very pleased with the content of my description of how Aldridge shot and Beasant saved. A truly historic moment at Wembley. Yet, inwardly, I was horrified that such a great side, as Liverpool were that year, were being beaten by a team I wouldn't dream of watching voluntarily. Perhaps, it was romantic, one of the best examples of that FA Cup magic, but I believed football, true football, was cheated by that Wimbledon win.

Now, a year on, Liverpool were on the verge of another Wembley appearance, and I had no reservations about their opponents that afternoon, or about those ahead in the final. Everton, Luton and Forest all played the game in a manner that I respected. Whoever would win at Hillsborough, or triumph at Wembley, I was likely to enjoy what I was about to describe. I had no idea of a possible sub-plot; that Liverpool had expressed reservations, as in 1988, about the accommodation set aside for their supporters. I was only vaguely aware that Forest, a club with a smaller support, had again been offered more seats and more room.

The couple of hours spent in the press room before kick-off were devoted, to a degree, to further preparation for the game, but mostly spent in idle chit-chat with fellow commentator Peter Jones, and summariser Jimmy Armfield. Sheffield Wednesday's hospitality towards the media was always very good and I don't think we made our way to the commentary position much before 2.45 p.m., by which time some had already died and more were about to.

As I sat down in my comfortable seat, my eyes surveyed the scene. The ground was already nearly full, not like these days when fans linger on by the food kiosks and beer outlets until the last possible moment. If you know your seat will be there, what's the point of rushing in and clambering for a better position? To this day, I'm still taken aback at how empty even a ground like Old Trafford looks ten minutes before the referee is due to blow his whistle, only to marvel at how quickly those seats fill up for the customary sell-out. Not so in 1989. You got there as early as you could to stand at your favourite spot, in front of or behind a crash barrier. Some preferred to be lower down, up against the fences, as close as possible to their heroes. Despite the scandalous misreports that suggested otherwise, many apparently emanating from the South Yorkshire Police, Liverpool fans weren't delaying their entry as late as possible, having a drink or otherwise. They made their way into the Leppings Lane end as quickly and as early as they could. Those policemen involved and Sheffield Wednesday Football Club must ask themselves, again and again, could they have done more to help. I fear the answer, particularly for the former, is yes.

I could see, looking to my left, that the central part of the terracing looked overcrowded, whereas both wings appeared to have more room available. But I didn't know the tragedy was already unfolding.

I started the commentary. To me, it was a thrill to be describing such an important occasion being played between two excellent teams. I remember getting into my stride very quickly and the opening moments flew by. I was concentrating on the football but I was also conscious of growing police activity to my left, towards Leppings Lane. Bruce Grobbelaar, defending the goal at that end, was more conscious still. He called the referee over. I admit I was confused; I was certain that it wasn't crowd trouble, I'd seen enough of that over the years to be able to understand the difference, but I didn't know what else it was. I only knew that the referee quickly stopped the game and took the players off. I continued commentating, trying to describe the scenes that were in front of me. The studio, though, unaware that this was anything other than a minor interruption, broke away from Hillsborough and went to the other semi-final at Villa Park.

I looked across, past Jimmy, to Peter. There was no point in us both just sitting there. Ignoring the producer, Pat Murphy, I told Peter that I was going down to the dressing-room area to find out what was happening. It was as if, however subconsciously, I had switched roles. Something was telling me there was no longer a need to commentate that afternoon, I must revert to being a news reporter again. It can only have been ten past three.

I went downstairs. Everyone seemed in a state of confusion, shock or panic. Policemen were rushing around. Though the players sat in their rooms, Kenny Dalglish and Brian Clough hovered outside, scratching around for information. They were told, as I heard, that there'd been a dreadful crush of people at the Leppings Lane end and it was certain there'd be casualties. Much of what followed was like being gripped in a nightmare that you couldn't wake up from. I couldn't tell you now the timescale, even the order in which things happened. They remain horrible flashes of memory on an afternoon that I'd rather forget.

I was still listening to the programme on headphones that stretched from our interview position a few yards from the away dressing-room. I heard a report by Peter. It's possible that I misheard what he said, but he gave me the impression that somehow hooligans were involved. I screamed at London: 'No! Tell Peter no! It's not hooliganism. It's not a riot. It's a crush. It's an accident. People are hurt. People are dying. It's not hooliganism.'

I heard of the first deaths. I reported them. I heard a rumour of how the gymnasium on the far side of the ground had been adopted as a temporary mortuary. I pulled a policeman aside. I don't remember his name now – I probably didn't know it then – and pressed him for casualty figures. I told him of how people were ringing the BBC, anxious to know what was happening to their sons and fathers, daughters and mothers, who were at the game. Liverpool fans who might be caught up in whatever had happened. Please, I said, get your superior officer to issue a telephone number that we might broadcast, that people might call.

From nowhere, Pat Murphy arrived. 'You're upsetting people,' he said. 'Back off.' I told Pat to go away and allow me to get on with the necessary job I was doing. He must have seen something in my eyes. I never saw him again that afternoon and have never spoken to him since about that day. The policeman came back and gave me the telephone number to broadcast.

The death toll mounted. As I reported on the figures and described how bodies were appearing in the players' tunnel aboard makeshift stretchers, Peter was up above commentating brilliantly on the horrendous scenes he was witnessing. It was his finest hour in broadcasting. I don't know how much it took out of him. He had also been at Heysel, and now there was Hillsborough. I've always believed that in the final year of his life – he died in April 1990 – Peter Jones was never quite the same. Never as buoyant, not as enthusiastic. I'm certain part of Jonesy died, too, that afternoon in South Yorkshire.

The programme lurched between Villa Park, where Mike Ingham and Bryon Butler had the impossible task of commentating on what they knew in the circumstances to be insignificant, and whatever we could provide from Hillsborough. I interviewed a Liverpool fan, a doctor, who was appalled at the absence of basic safety equipment. I spoke to the FA secretary, Graham Kelly. We were handed the latest casualty figures as the interview was going on. Graham was crying as he read them out. So was I.

It must have been two and a half hours before I returned to the commentary position. Peter was still there. I listened as he spoke magnificently into the six o'clock news on Radio 4. True news reporters were already on site and once Peter finished his piece, we were free to go.

We said little to each other. I knew he was heading for the railway station and I was going to the Crucible Theatre, where the Embassy World Professional Snooker Championship was under way. I was to be the reporter there for the next seventeen days. I hadn't even begun to think about the absurdity of my going there in such circumstances. Whatever, I told Peter I would take him to the station.

Still we said little. I drove. He sat in the passenger seat alongside me. We were both crying. As the car stopped outside the station, Peter shook my hand: 'Goodnight, Alan, see you very soon. Look after yourself.' He headed for the next train to London.

That evening was surreal. The snooker went on around me, but I was oblivious to it. Writers and broadcasters, most of whom were dear friends, approached me frequently but warily. Was I all right? Could they do anything to help? Could they get me another drink? I drank a lot that evening and deep into the night, enough alcohol to have seen me pass out. Somehow, I didn't. No amount could make me forget, erase the hurt. And I wasn't injured. I wasn't part of the casualty list that lengthened as the night wore on.

The next morning, I made my way from the flat I was renting in Sheffield for the tournament back to the Crucible. I rang London.

Had anyone spoken to Peter? Did they know how he was? I rang his home and spoke to his wife. She told me that he was still very upset but he'd be fine. I rang London again. They asked if I wanted to go home, to get away from Sheffield. I said I didn't know. I had a feeling that working on might prove therapeutic. Could I think about it?

By Monday, I had decided to carry on at the snooker but now I had another decision to make. Mike Lewis, Head of Sport, rang to explain how they'd been thinking of the week ahead. Sheffield United were due to play Leyton Orient at Bramall Lane on the Saturday. The match was going ahead and would be the first played in the city since the tragedy. They needed Peter or me to be there. Would I go? Would I think about it? It was such a difficult thing to do, but would I? I suppose there really was no decision to make. Of course, I had to go.

The snooker really helped in the days leading up to the United game. It was such hard work over long hours but it distracted my mind as much as it could be distracted. But I still dreaded the thought of what lay ahead at Bramall Lane.

I arrived very early, around midday, and drove into my allotted car park space at the back of the main stand. I knew I didn't have to go in just then but I couldn't anyway. My hands were shaking. All I could think about was Hillsborough. I noticed police arriving. They were walking along the lane by the main entrance, laughing and joking. How could they? They were South Yorkshire police. Some of them must surely have been at Hillsborough. How could they?

Eventually, I went into the ground and up to the press room. There was the usual small talk: who'd be playing, who was injured, could United get promotion? I heard it all but listened to none of it. I knew I wasn't there for football reasons.

The kick-off was delayed until six minutes past three. All the players were grouped in a circle, heads bowed. I stood in the press box. There was silence except for the church bells that, as arranged, rang throughout Sheffield. I broke down. I was in a state of collapse. I've no idea what I said in my reports or what happened in the game. It didn't matter.

That night, I drove through the Peak District towards home in Macclesfield, where I was planning to stay the night before returning to the snooker. I listened to *Sports Report* along the way and stopped the car just west of Castleton to listen to Bryon Butler's report from Anfield, where thousands had laid wreaths and scarves and tributes, where a service had been held. Bryon's report was one of the most skilfully written and delivered pieces that I've ever heard.

Life had to go on. The funerals took place, attended by Liverpool players who also visited those lying injured in hospitals. My admiration for them, and particularly Kenny Dalglish, is limitless. I cannot begin to understand how they managed to sustain the mental strength to get through all that and then find the motivation to play football again that season. It was difficult enough for Peter and me merely commentating. The rearranged semi-final at Old Trafford was especially difficult. I'm sure it was the same for the players and worse still for the spectators. It was something we all needed to get through.

Ironically, I didn't commentate on the final. At the time, Mike Ingham and I rotated the role as cup final co-commentator to Peter Jones. It was Mike's turn. Strangely, though, I didn't mind. I wouldn't have been able to cope as well as Peter did. When Gerry Marsden stood on the pitch before kick-off to sing 'You'll Never Walk Alone' I found it so upsetting that I had to leave our commentary box, high among the girders of the Wembley roof, and find a quiet spot to shed further tears.

It was a relief when the game ended. It wasn't as if I felt I could leave all the painful memories behind. There have been many times since that I've found myself crying, remembering what happened on that April day. When, for example, my wife tried to persuade me not to watch the excellent Jimmy McGovern drama-documentary. She knew it would upset me and she was right. However, with the conclusion of that season's FA Cup competition, I knew that at least one chapter had closed on the Hillsborough disaster. More would certainly be written but they'd look forward, not back, embracing the lessons that had to be learnt.

What has happened in the decade or so since Hillsborough, in terms of the quality of English grounds, particularly in the Premiership, and how spectators are treated, is little short of astounding. Most of the changes were necessary and obvious, but I doubt they'd have taken place as quickly as they did without the impetus brought about by the FA Cup semi-final tragedy.

Lord Taylor's report instituted a revolution. The idea that no fan should have to stand to watch professional football in England hasn't yet been enforced throughout the game, and I would agree with those who argue that it shouldn't be enforced at all levels. That is unnecessary. It would place too heavy a financial burden on lower-division clubs already struggling to make ends meet and the safety concerns that applied at Hillsborough are inapplicable in arenas where they're accustomed to crowds of only a few thousand. But I have no sympathy whatsoever with those who argue for a return to standing enclosures in the Premiership.

I well remember the days when you stood behind the goal that your team was attacking in the first half and then changed ends at the interval, passing opposing fans and swapping banter with them. Could anyone seriously envisage that happening today at any significant level of the game? In terms of safety or preventing the hooliganism that has never gone away from our sport? I don't believe so.

I detest those who arrogantly persist in exercising what they perceive to be a right to stand at a game. You know the sort. They climb up on their seat in front of you and then force you to do the same. Stewards and members of the public who try to get them to sit down are shouted down. It's horrible. Can you imagine what would happen if someone fell over? Remember, there are no safety barriers in these stands. The result could be catastrophic and I applaud, in particular, the stance of Manchester United in trying to eradicate the problem at Old Trafford. I would say to those who don't want to sit down, find some other sport to threaten with your anti-social behaviour.

It was fascinating, but worrying, being in Rio de Janeiro for the inaugural FIFA Club World Championship to see how the local organisers had tarted up the decaying Maracana stadium as the main venue. It would certainly have failed any meaningful health and safety inspection in most European countries. They'd installed over 60,000 seats, most of them in that cheap half-baked manner of hammering a bit of plastic on to a concrete terrace. It brought the capacity of the historic setting down to just over 100,000 and it was resented by the local Brazilian fans who are accustomed to standing and jumping about. It didn't stop them doing precisely that during the tournament. They simply ignored the seats. Certainly, it contributed to the atmosphere in the games that drew big crowds, but it was an accident waiting to happen. I would have hated to have been among them and I wouldn't consider exposing my wife and family to such threatening circumstances.

Football has, since Hillsborough, become much more family orientated. Is that so bad? Why shouldn't there be family enclosures? Most times, they're in the less desirable parts of the ground, tucked away around a corner flag. Why shouldn't they occupy more central positions? Surely not because of those who still think they can stand and swear as they have always done?

I accept that the changing nature of the football fan has led to a more dispassionate atmosphere at many stadia. Isn't that a small price to pay for knowing that you're now more likely to leave the ground with all your limbs intact? And, anyway, this change in atmosphere is due to other factors as well. The fewer seats made available for away supporters has been crucial. There is bound to be less noise at a ground when the support is overwhelmingly for the home team. Think how much better the atmosphere is when it's an FA Cup tie and the away team is guaranteed a substantial number of tickets. Perhaps security may have to be increased but what a difference it makes. Oh, that it applied to all games.

Ninety-six people died needlessly at Hillsborough and I will struggle to forgive those that I hold chiefly responsible: the police. But those deaths left behind a positive legacy for the game as a whole. We watch games in a better and safer environment today. Why did it take a tragedy to happen to provoke the change?

CHAPTER TEN

THE BEST SEAT IN THE HOUSE

'A tough life, eh?' they say to me. 'You're paid to be there *and* you have the best seat in the house!' Overwhelmingly, of course, they're right.

Mike Ingham and I spent most of the 1994 World Cup the width of a continent apart. He stayed on the eastern side of the United States whereas I was based on the west coast. We didn't meet up until a couple of days before the final, which was being held at the Rose Bowl in Pasadena, a suburb of the sprawling mess that is Los Angeles. Almost the first thing Mike asked me about was the commentary position. I told him that I might have hand-picked it myself. It was that good.

It had the perfect elevation for commentary, not so low that you lose perspective, not so high that as in the Nou Camp, you feel you're watching Subbuteo. It was positioned directly over the halfway line and little more than ten yards behind a podium on which stood the World Cup trophy itself. You felt as if you could reach out and touch it, as Dunga did once Brazil had beaten Italy on penalties in that dreadfully disappointing game.

Yet the Rose Bowl commentary position had a geographic penalty all of its own. The blistering Californian sun shone directly down over our heads in a stadium that offers no cover. There is hardly ever any rain. Why would you need a roof? But that meant there were two serious problems for those who had to commentate on matches being played there. First, you needed protection from the sun. Second, the television monitors that were available as back-up proved useless because of the resultant glare.

The American organisers, recognising problem two, provided large cardboard boxes to help cover the TV screens. I solved problem one by accepting the box given to me and wearing it on my head. It wasn't exactly a fashion statement worthy of Calvin Klein but it was far less silly to look at than the ridiculous green sombrero which John Motson took to wearing at the ground.

For many years, people believed that Wembley offered the best in everything as far as football is concerned. It's now in the process of being rebuilt. Thank goodness. Recently, it had become a dump of a stadium, its passing mourned only by those who remembered how good it was as opposed to the reality of what it had become. I hated the cost, the smells and, most of all, the inaccessibility. Yes, you could park easily, but think how long it took to get away from the place. Wembley is a site for a national stadium which may have made sense eighty years ago but doesn't today. No matter how good the new structure is there will still be a problem getting to and from it for anyone who doesn't live in or near to London. Much better to have gone to the M42 around Birmingham; good roads, rail and plane links, plenty of room to park and nearer the centre of the country. Anyway . . .

The one thing I shall miss about Wembley was the excellence of the BBC Radio commentary box. We had a wonderful position, an eagle's eyrie slung beneath the roof. We actually had to walk through girders to reach it. Once there, the view was magnificently uninterrupted. If a commentator got it wrong at Wembley then he usually had only himself to blame. However, there was one important deficiency. You couldn't see the Royal Box. We were too far forward. This meant that to describe the presentation of a trophy, the commentator had to rely on a television monitor.

In 1993, Arsenal beat Sheffield Wednesday in the League Cup final. I 'finished' the game and you may remember the joyous Gunner celebrations at the climax during which the captain, Tony Adams, lifted colleague Steve Morrow off his feet and then dropped him, breaking the Ulsterman's shoulder. Looking on, you couldn't tell the extent of the injury but Morrow wasn't moving, the stretcher was on the pitch, and clearly the presentation ceremony needed to be delayed.

ITV was covering the game, providing the pictures for the monitor in our commentary box. The director must have decided that the call of commercials was too strong to resist and took a break in the transmission from Wembley in order to show a few advertisements. What I didn't know then, but soon found out, was that he'd also decided to let the presentation happen during this break, record it, and then play it in on video later as if it was live. I only grasped what was going on when Tony Adams was given the instruction, shrugged his shoulders, leaving Morrow with the damaged one, and led the remaining Arsenal players up the steps towards the Royal Box and out of my sight. When the monitor should have been showing me pictures of the cup being lifted, I was really watching an ad for washing-up liquid! In commentary parlance, I had no option but to 'busk' the whole ceremony because I didn't see a thing. I've never quite forgiven ITV.

★ ★ ★

Many commentary positions are not remotely as good as they're perceived to be by the public. You'd think that Manchester United, one of the greatest clubs in the world with one of the best grounds in the world, would offer excellent facilities for the media, but it doesn't. The Old Trafford press box, from which we commentate, is far too small and it's seriously cramped. Once you sit down, it's impossible to move unless everybody else does.

However, United is far from being among the worst in the Premiership. Indeed, they're one of the best! Tottenham is a disgrace. The press box and commentary position is set low to the right of the players' tunnel, immediately in front of the pitch. The camber of the playing surface means that you can't tell if a foul is committed inside or outside the penalty area or whether a pass has gone over the far touchline. You can't see, from our position, at least one and usually two of the corner flags.

Newcastle is fine except you're even more hemmed into your seat than at Old Trafford; if the fans in the row in front stand up, you don't see anything at all; and if it rains, you get soaked (the main stand didn't have a roof for the whole of 1999–2000). Away the lads!

In contrast, Arsenal offers a wonderful position: the front of the stand, reasonable access and a terrific view. So, too, does West Ham. I love doing a game at Upton Park. You have elevation, but you're very close to the touchline, so you almost feel as if you're close enough to play.

I don't know what the problem is. Perhaps, and I fear this is the case, most clubs merely suffer the media and really couldn't care less about their discomfort. This suspicion is supported by the relative lack of consultation that seems to take place when a new stadium is being built. 'Get those executive boxes right, and make sure there are enough bars and fast food outlets. Toilets? Yeah, we'd better have some of those. The media? They'll have to go there and lump it.'

Sunderland's Stadium of Light is a good example. It looks magnificent and has a wonderful atmosphere, almost as good as Roker Park was. What a shame they didn't think harder about media requirements. The position is too low and only a midget could find it comfortable getting in and out of the woefully inadequate seats. I'll be surprised if UEFA don't criticise the arrangements should Sunderland play in European competition soon, especially if it's the Champions League.

To be fair, you have to excuse the older grounds that have merely been refurbished. They are probably incapable of offering decent media facilities. They were built at a time when it truly didn't matter.

There are exceptions. I regret that Norwich City aren't in the Premiership. They clearly gave great thought to their press area; excellent seats, plenty of room to move around in and a good bench to work on. And when Leicester City built their magnificent new stand at Filbert Street they did talk to people to gauge how to balance what was needed with what was possible. The facilities there are superb.

You'll notice I've picked out two smaller clubs. Too many of the bigger ones obviously think they don't have to try. All of them should be packed off to the United States to see how sports should treat broadcasters and reporters. Still, it frequently gives me something to moan about and, boy, haven't I had cause to moan about facilities over the years!

CHAPTER ELEVEN

LIFE ON THE ROAD

The number of commentaries I do every season, usually more than a hundred, doesn't equate to the number of days spent doing them. There is an enormous amount of travelling involved, even for games in England, and for those abroad there is the day spent getting there, the day of the match itself and the day to return home. Those who don't understand the business don't believe it but, trust me, the so-called glamour of travel soon wears off.

I own two passports, one to use in case the other needs to sit in some foreign embassy awaiting a visa. A flick through either of them would reveal the countless destinations I've been to, no doubt provoking considerable jealousy, but they wouldn't necessarily reveal the hassles involved. One of my passports, for example, has five Turkish visas in it. Each of them cost £5, which you have to pay in cash at the frontier. I always thought that suspicious though, in retrospect, it was a warning of things to come. There is no foreign venue that I like less than Turkey.

My first visit, with the Republic of Ireland, was innocent enough. It was a game in Izmir, part of the Irish build-up to the 1990 World Cup and, save for a probably paranoid notion of feeling threatened each time I left my hotel, the trip was memorable only for the poverty of the fixture itself. It was easily one of the worst games I've ever seen. There wasn't a single shot on target during the ninety minutes. Each of the reporters was desperately scrambling to find something to say or write about afterwards. Unfortunately, Jack Charlton, the Republic's manager, who was always good for a quote, went missing. Perhaps even he was at a loss for words. It was so bad that one national newspaper writer exclaimed: 'Don't worry. I'll make up the quotes!' Mischievously, another reporter partly filled his column with the story and it nearly led to blows between the two of them the next day.

As I say, my nervousness at being outside the confines of the hotel was almost certainly irrational but my next visit to Turkey, and to Izmir, this time with England, saw my fiction turn into fact. This wasn't a friendly, it was a European Championship qualifier in May 1991, won by a solitary goal from Dennis Wise. The locals did their best to intimidate. I will never forget watching, as the England players stepped down off the coach, adults and children spitting at them from a balcony. During the game, Mike Ingham, Ray Clemence and I had to shelter beside a wall to evade a fusillade of stones, bottles and fruit being thrown towards the area where members of the Football Association were sitting. It was horrible; I couldn't wait to get out. And I dreaded the thought of ever returning. Sadly, I haven't been that lucky.

Istanbul was the setting for Manchester United's Champions League game against Galatasaray. Thanks to some stupidly insensitive reporting in the Sunday newspapers the weekend before, we were greeted at the airport by the sign 'WELCOME TO HELL' . . . and that's what it felt like.

Now I know many people will tell you that Turkey is a wonderful place to visit, and that Istanbul with its Blue Mosque is the jewel in the crown. Perhaps. But they weren't on that trip. I can't tell you what it was like for the players but I have never felt as intimidated in my life. It was as if we'd flown into a war zone. Armed troops escorted us to the stadium and were meant to protect the party. They didn't stop Eric Cantona being assaulted in the tunnel after the match; they may even have taken part. Mike Ingham and I were so shaken by the whole experience that on a return to the city, we refused to leave the hotel until the game, and only because of the game.

As well, deliberately or otherwise, it's my experience that the broadcasting facilities in Turkey are primitive. This time United played Fenerbahce in the Champions League. The atmosphere wasn't quite as hostile as against Galatasaray though the man on the tannoy system spent the whole of the match trying to incite the crowd. Fenerbahce were fined by UEFA as a result.

We were almost too busy with our own problems to notice. Despite ample warning of our basic requirements (there had been no problems with the facilities which the BBC had made available to the Turkish broadcasters at Old Trafford), we found that our circuit at the Fenerbahce stadium consisted of bare wires. No microphones, no headsets, nothing. Oh, and no seats either! We had to commentate on a telephone that we managed to borrow. I couldn't hear what Mark Lawrenson said. He couldn't hear me either. We just passed the phone between us whenever it felt right. I was sitting on a concrete step and I couldn't see anything of the goal to my right. And this was the Champions League!

One journalistic colleague, not in the BBC, found the perfect way out of his own dissatisfaction with the problems of working in Turkey. He was so critical of the situation in newspaper articles that the Turkish government banned him from returning. I swear he thought he'd died and gone to heaven.

Sadly, UEFA seems either unable or unwilling to take action against Turkish football. Look what happened when Leeds went to

Istanbul in the UEFA Cup and two fans were stabbed to death. Galatasaray's behaviour afterwards was quite appalling. The club refused to accept that they had any culpability for the violence committed by their supporters. They then had the nerve to want the second leg played at a neutral venue. All the while, they were manoeuvring the worrying situation to try to gain the maximum advantage to enhance their chances of reaching the final. Typical. Typical of UEFA, too, to punish them with a feather duster.

Turkey isn't alone on the list of places that I'd prefer not to go to. I remember during the 1992 European Championship attending a press conference in Gothenburg promoting Morocco's bid to host the 1998 World Cup. I still have the badges that were given out. It was only six years later, a month before France 98, when I realised what a narrow escape we'd had.

England played some World Cup warm-up games in Casablanca. I thought at the time that the Football Association had been rather rude to the Moroccan hosts by insisting on England staying in their Spanish hideaway at La Manga and merely flying in and out for the matches. It was, they argued, the sort of regime they were planning for the World Cup itself. However, it also had the fortunate by-product of avoiding Casablanca. What a dump! The people are incredibly friendly but I found the venue a nightmare. We stayed at what we were told was a good hotel. There were pigeons lying dead in the swimming pool the whole of our stay.

We attended a party thrown by the then England sponsors, Green Flag. It was staged at what was reckoned to be the best hotel in the city. The buffet looked wonderfully attractive until I saw the head chef mixing up the chicken kebab meat with his bare hands. I gave it a miss.

Organisation? What organisation? They had no accreditation ready for Terry Butcher. It was nearing kick-off time in England's first game. I tried to persuade those issuing the passes that they were turning away someone who'd captained his country. Others around vouched for Terry's identity. Reluctantly, they conjured up photographic accreditation for him. Only when we tried to reach the commentary positions did we discover what they'd done. They'd put Terry down on the list as part of the England squad! He couldn't reach the broadcasting area but he could walk straight into the dressing-room. Thank goodness it was just a friendly match. Honestly, I can't imagine the utter chaos there'd be if Morocco ever got to host the big event. Not even FIFA could be so stupid as to give it to them.

Kiev is another dodgy venue. I don't doubt the beauty of parts of the city or denigrate its efforts to escape the greyness of its communist past. But there are problems. Going with Arsenal to play Dynamo, the club warned us that we'd have to take our own food. Not the best of starts, particularly when the distance involved entails staying two nights.

Dutifully, I went to Marks and Spencer. A couple of chicken sandwiches (why must the sell-by date always be the next day?), two pasta salads, fruit bowls and bottled water. I needed to lose weight anyway. I also visited the off-licence to buy two bottles of red wine. We'd all agreed to do so. If you couldn't eat the food or drink the water, how could you risk the local plonk?

The first evening, the Monday night, the BBC party of producer Charlotte Nicol, summariser John McGovern, Mike Ingham and I set up camp in my cramped quarters. Lottie took the floor, Mike the solitary chair, and John and I each lounged on sagging single beds. The hotel was 'minus two stars'. Mind you, the company was great and everybody was feeling a lot better after sharing a few bottles of wine. Now for the food. I opened a sandwich, slightly worried that it felt warm. It didn't smell that good either after the long flight to the

Ukrainian capital in a less-than-cold aircraft cabin.

Mike fancied one of the tins of tuna that he'd brought with him and left to fetch it from his room. He was less cheerful when he returned having discovered that his can-opener had broken. Two days to survive, plenty of tinned food but nothing to open it with. There was nothing else to be done; he decided to go to reception and fall on their mercy.

Mike returned, slightly ashen-faced, a few minutes later. When he got out of the lift at the ground floor, tin of tuna held to the fore, he almost walked straight into three of the most beautiful women he'd ever seen. 'Oh, I'm sorry,' he said.

'Hello,' one of them replied. Mike couldn't help but smile back. They were being friendly and the red wine had him in a very good mood, despite the can-opener problem.

'You like us?' another of the girls asked.

Puzzled, but wishing not to offend, Mike replied: 'Yes, of course I like you.'

'You want us?' said the third.

Now Mike was catching on. 'NO! NO!' said Mike, pointing to his wedding ring. 'Me happily married man!' He jumped back into the lift as quickly as he could. Stuff the tuna!

Mike's brief, unwarranted, encounter with those ladies of the night is sadly all too typical in countries like Ukraine. There is so little work for people. Not unreasonably in the circumstances, they'll do anything they can to earn money. I remember travelling with Mike in a taxi in Moscow discussing whether we'd buy some caviar to take home. Suddenly, the car screamed to a stop. The driver jumped out and pulled open our door. 'Come look what I've got in the boot,' he said. We hadn't even known he spoke English.

I went back to Kiev later that season to commentate on the European Cup semi-final between Dynamo and Bayern Munich. I travelled on my own with Swissair through Zurich and, I must admit, I was more than a little wary on my arrival in Kiev. First of all, not being on an organised trip, how was I to get in from the airport? There are no official taxis. I thought I'd play it smart. I declined each and every offer of 'taxi?' making my way towards the exit. All the while I was looking for someone semi-official. I thought I'd found him. 'Taxi?' I asked.

'Of course, sir. Where to?' I told him and we negotiated a fee in US dollars, whereupon he handed me on to 'Dimitri'. 'Dimitri' spoke reasonable English. I asked if he could give me a receipt. This was clearly a problem for 'Dimitri'. He introduced me to 'Ivan'. 'Ivan' said he would be able to give me a receipt and 'Would you now please follow me?' I was clearly in the hands of the local taxi mafia but what choice did I have?

'Ivan' drove me into Kiev in a battered, evil-smelling Skoda. I didn't think we'd make it. Worse, I had a suspicion I wasn't being taken anywhere near my hotel. My paranoia was rife.

We pulled up at a building that looked nothing like any hotel, more of an office block, but 'Ivan' assured me it was the Kreschatik. Sheepishly, I got out of the car, not so much thinking I'd reached the hotel, more that probably I now had a decent chance of making a run for it. But, actually, it was the Kreschatik. What it wasn't was like any other hotel I'd ever stayed at before.

A woman sat alone at a desk. Yes, she had my name but No, she wouldn't give me a key before I'd paid the full amount for both nights – in cash, no travellers' cheques or credit cards. I unburdened myself of every dollar and deutschmark that I possessed. I just made it.

The room was unbelievably bad. I made my mind up there and then that I would sleep, fully clothed, in what passed for a chair. I dreaded the thought of what diseases I might pick up if I dared to crawl under the bed-sheets. A wise decision.

How would I survive this? I tried to make contact with the colleagues I knew would also have the misfortune of unpacking in this forsaken place. They were nowhere to be found so, in desperation, I retreated to what passed for reception. I'd already discovered that the hotel didn't have a restaurant or a bar.

Suddenly, I detected American voices. There must have been thirty of them. This wasn't a Hilton or a Hyatt. What were they doing here? At that moment, Roy Calley, the producer, walked through the front door. I greeted him as you would the only other survivor after a nuclear war. Why are we in this dump? Who are all these Americans? He sat me down. He couldn't answer the first question but he now had a good idea of the explanation to the second.

The Kreschatik is the Kiev headquarters of an organisation called 'European Connections'. Lonely American men, mostly old, mostly sick if you ask me, make excursions to the Ukrainian capital in search of a young, beautiful partner to take back to a wond'rful life in the good ol' USA . . . at least that's what they tell these girls.

I spent a lot of time in that reception during the trip observing what went on. It made me want to find a machine-gun to eliminate these sordid representatives of the self-anointed greatest democracy on the planet. Girls and women would arrive, clearly dressed in their Sunday best clothes, and they'd be examined like cattle to see if they'd fit what was required. I watched one American, he must have been around sixty-five. He wore a stetson, smoked a huge cigar and his waistline bore the fruits of too many beers and hot dogs. He had his arm around a beautiful girl who couldn't have been more than twenty.

'I live in Colorado,' he said, 'where all the movie stars live. We go skiing in the mountains during the winter. It's really beautiful. You'll lurve it.'

I got up before I threw up. I left the building to try to find some fresh air. When I returned, they were still there. Something was going wrong. The girl was crying. 'What is it?' he said. 'Is it my having children that bothers you? Don't worry, everything will be all right.'

I overheard another American. He was discussing his 'date' of last night. 'Boy, did she rip me off . . . the meal cost seventy dollars and she asked for a pack of cigarettes as well! I don't know, she looked well enough, but you can get girls just as good back home.'

I discovered – they didn't exactly hide it – that many of these visitors came for a couple of weeks, some for a month, 'road-testing' a different girl every night, sometimes all night. It wasn't costing them much. So what if they didn't find anybody worth persisting with. Damn the commitment, just have fun! I will never, ever, return to that hotel and preferably not to Kiev either. It was the European equivalent of Bangkok. Cheap sex for tourists.

Thankfully, I haven't come across any hotel remotely similar in England. Indeed, I stay in far fewer hotels than you'd imagine. My wife, Brenda, might beg to differ but I never spend a minute longer away from home than I have to. Hotels and strange beds hold little attraction for me. Wherever the game, if it's possible and sensible for me to get home that evening, even if it's early in the morning, I always head for the car and drive up the motorway towards Cheshire.

Sometimes, I admit, it's not the brightest thing to do. The adrenaline that's still flowing after commentating on a game or presenting a programme eventually wears out. That's when you have to open all the car windows and turn up the stereo to try to stay awake. It doesn't always work. I swear there have been times that I've fallen asleep at the wheel, only to be jolted awake frightened by what's happened or by what might have happened. I've been lucky. My colleague Ian Brown, like me anxious to get home, nodded off on the way back to Cardiff from Newcastle and woke up after his car had hit a motorway crash barrier. He might have been killed.

One night, I was commentating at the Dell. It was midwinter and the weather forecast threatened patchy fog on the journey back north. I should have gone to a hotel. However, the thought of roads clear of traffic, the thought of sleeping in my own bed, urged me towards the car. It was a very big mistake.

Everything was clear until I drove on to the A34. It was like being on an aeroplane flying into a bank of cloud. Suddenly, I could see nothing around me. I thought then of pulling over and trying to find a place to stay. But where? It was near midnight, I didn't know the area. I decided to carry on, hoping the fog would break. Somehow, hogging the broken white line of the lane, I drove slowly north. Past Oxford, eventually on to the M40, creeping northwards.

By the time I reached the M42, south of Birmingham, the fog was beginning to thin and I felt the worst was over. On the contrary, it was still to come. Approaching the Hilton service area on the M6, it was a matter of clinging on to the fog lights of the vehicle in front and trusting that, way ahead, someone knew where they were going. I knew that all I had to do was drive slowly, 'safely' being out of the question, and eventually I'd reach the Sandbach turnoff, my normal motorway exit heading north. There were, however, two problems. One, the fog was that bad it was really difficult to see the signs; two, I knew that if it remained foggy, the twisting road through Congleton to Macclesfield would be too dangerous to attempt. I'd end up in a ditch.

I decided to exit two junctions later, at Knutsford. That was a straighter road home and I knew the route just as well. Honestly, I barely made out the motorway sign and, so disorientated had I become, I nearly took the wrong turning off the roundabout at the top of the junction. I'd been driving for hours in this state and it

While some managers may be unduly prickly, Jack Charlton was one of the most friendly and welcoming characters I've had to deal with. (*Colorsport*)

Gary Lineker gets his own back by scribbling over this photograph, 'This man publicly criticised my haircut.' Sorry, Gary, but I still think I win!

With Jimmy Armfield before the 1994 World Cup final in Pasadena. For a man who has given so much to football, his honour in 2000 was strangely delayed. (*Popperfoto*)

In the commentary box ahead of the World Cup semi-final in 1998 with Terry Butcher and my partner in crime Mike Ingham.

Some ruins in Pompeii: here I am with Bob Shennan, controller of Radio 5 Live, and former England goalkeeper Ray Clemence during Italia 90.

With Graeme Souness for my Friday night *5 Live* programme. Not all managers have been so accommodating.

Mike Ingham and I with Scotland manager Craig Brown during the Club World Championship.

My job has given me some great opportunities for travel. *Left*: I try on all the hats I can in Moscow's Red Square while (*below*) this army of journalists was just the sort of thing the Great Wall of China was built to protect the country from. *Left to right (back)*: Mike Ingham, Henry Winter, Steve Curry, Gary Newbon and me. *Front*: Harry Harris and Neil Harmon.

wasn't getting any easier. Indeed, I was beginning to panic. I felt my way through Knutsford. I couldn't see it; I felt it. There were ten miles to go but I was damned if I was going to give up now.

As I left the town, I realised the slight assistance afforded by the street lights had now gone. I was truly on my own. Visibility must have been down to a couple of yards. I was petrified about driving into a parked car and, though I thought about doing so, I couldn't pull my car over for fear that somebody eventually would drive into me. Instead, I moved the car slightly nearer to the centre of the road and deliberately bumped the wheels over the cats' eyes, as if driving on one of those kiddies' racetracks.

Yet, amazingly, however bad the fog had been, it was getting worse. I simply had to stop, I was so frightened. I remembered there was a caravan dealership on the right-hand side, a couple of miles outside Knutsford. Even though I was so close to home, I decided I would try to pull in there and sleep in the car for the rest of the night. It was impossible. I passed the opportunity by without seeing it.

Suddenly, miraculously, I emerged from the fog. I could see ahead its bank, hanging no more than ten feet above the road. I put my foot down and scurried the four miles home not knowing whether to laugh or cry.

Thankfully, Brenda had slept through my crisis, oblivious to the dangers I had been driving through. There was no fog over Macclesfield. I drank the largest brandy I'd ever seen and slipped into bed around 4.30 a.m.

I use the train when I can but the route to London is unreliable; and I can't get a train home after eight o'clock at night. So most of the time I drive, doing around 25,000 miles a year on business. At least I can be cushioned by air conditioning and the CD player, even sitting in the notorious motorway area around Birmingham where rush hour lasts from 7 a.m. until 7 p.m. But when I was on BBC staff, driving was far less luxurious.

Generally, the BBC allocates staff vehicles for two reasons: either as an unashamed perk to management or to its high-mileage reporters and producers – as a way of the BBC saving money, but not for the benefit of its staff. I had no real complaints with my car then, but as a freelance I can now drive in something more comfortable.

Driving home one Saturday night from Hereford, where I had been commentating on their FA Cup tie against Tottenham Hotspur, proved memorable for two reasons. First, I had to pull into a service area on the M5 to ring in to *Six-0-Six*. A Spurs supporter had berated me for constantly giving scorelines from other cup-ties instead of concentrating on describing the fortunes of his beloved team. David Mellor hadn't explained that I was acting on the instructions of a producer and that, particularly on third round day, we were obliged to tell people what was going on in the thirty or so other games. I phoned to put him and the supporter right.

When I got home, I put the car in the garage. Outside, it was a wild night, weatherwise, but I could distinctly hear an odd whistling sound. I couldn't track it down. I suspected it was the central heating boiler and cursed my typical good fortune in having such a problem on a Saturday evening when there wasn't a cat in hell's chance of getting a plumber out. At least the radiators were still working.

I got up early the next morning to drive to Derby for County's cup meeting with Leeds at the old Baseball Ground. I heard the whistling sound as soon as I entered the garage. Damn, it hadn't gone away. The papers hadn't arrived so I stopped at a newsagent's to get something to read for when I got to Derby. To my surprise, the whistling had come with me. It wasn't the central heating that was the problem, it was the car. I opened the bonnet. The whistling was more pronounced but I'm no mechanic. I could only assume I'd driven the whole way home from Hereford with this going on, but the car was driving fine, it would just have to wait until I got it to the local garage on the Monday morning.

Arriving at the car park by the Baseball Ground, I wound down the window to speak to the steward. Before I could say anything, he said: 'You know there's a funny whistling sound coming from your car?' Yes, I knew, and I explained what little I knew about it, that it wasn't affecting the performance of the car and that it would be sorted the following morning. 'Don't worry, it's not a bomb.'

Jimmy Armfield, the match summariser, pulled up in the space beside me. He tapped the window: 'Greenie, do you know there's a funny sound coming from your car?' Another explanation. We sat having a chat together for a while and then, as we left the car park to go into the ground, I reminded the steward not to worry about the noise. I forgot about it. The game made it easy to forget. It was a terrific match, full of goals and incident-packed.

It wasn't long after I'd picked up commentary from Jon Champion during the second half. I was describing a Leeds attack that had broken down when I heard the distinctive 'bing-bong' of the tannoy system. Though I was talking, I could make out quite clearly what the man on the public address was saying: 'Would the owner of a red Peugeot, registration number M289 LYO, please return immediately to his car?' I had countless thoughts in that split second. I'd told the steward what was wrong. What can have happened now? It must be serious. Could the car be on fire?

'Jim,' I said. 'That's my car he's talking about.'

'Yes,' came the reply, 'and we know what the problem is.'

'Aye [and I explained there'd been this funny noise], but what if it's something else now? I'll have to go and check. Jon, would you take up the commentary again?'

I clambered out of my seat. The press box was in fits of laughter.

Many of the guys listen on radios at the same time they're watching the game. They knew where I was going. I ran out of the ground and across the road to the car park. I saw a steward and explained that the car was mine. What's the problem? 'Well, there's a funny noise coming from the car.'

'What are you talking about? I told your colleague all about it. Don't you know I'm supposed to be commentating in there [pointing to the ground]?'

He explained that the stewards changed shifts at half-time so that they could each get to see something of the game. He apologised that the message hadn't been passed on.

I ran back into the ground and sat down. The laughter had hardly stopped. I looked across to Jon: 'Anything happen while I've been away?' He shook his head. 'Good. Throw-in to Derby, near side of the field, their left in this second half . . .'

Radio 5 publicity was on the phone by the time I returned home. The *Sun* was looking for a few quotes. What? About my stupid car? Have they nothing better to write about? Amazingly, only the *Guardian* and the *Independent* had the sense not to write about my car the following morning! Every other national newspaper devoted column inches to the story of the commentary that was interrupted while the commentator responded to a tannoy announcement asking him to return to his vehicle. *The Times* gave it seven paragraphs. The *Daily Telegraph* reported it and there was a follow-up piece in the same newspaper the following Saturday. Chris Evans, then doing the breakfast show on Radio 1, dedicated his programme to me and replayed the whole affair on tape. Serves the BBC right.

P.S. The whistling sound was traced to a fault in the alarm system.

CHAPTER TWELVE

FROM GREEN TO GREEN

As you've read, there are moments when I have to remind myself that I'm not dreaming, that I'm actually witnessing, close up, great sporting events and, I'm ashamed to admit it, being paid to be there. Some stick in my mind, often as a portent of things to come.

In 1983, during a practice round for the Open Golf Championship, I remember walking down the fairway of the fifth hole at Royal Birkdale a matter of yards behind Jack Nicklaus. I heard someone call out to me from behind the spectator ropes and turned to see Kenny Dalglish waving. He was playing for Liverpool at the time. I thought: 'What's this? He's a football superstar and he can't get closer than fifty yards. Me? I could touch Nicklaus. I could talk to him!' Of course, I did neither, but you get my drift.

I was only helping to supply preview material for the golf producer that year and only because the Open was taking place on my 'patch', but it certainly whetted my appetite to become more fully involved in the sport. The venues between 1984 and 1987 were St Andrews,

Royal St George's, Turnberry and Muirfield. I wasn't required and watched enviously from afar.

In 1988, though, the championship returned to the north-west, to Royal Lytham & St Annes, and Gordon Turnbull once more asked me to help out. I was chuffed to bits, especially as my help extended far further than either of us anticipated.

My initial role was as interviewer. I stood behind the eighteenth green, close to the scorer's cabin, and approached the golfers once the necessary formalities had been completed. I talked to everyone that moved and some made a particular impression on me. Curtis Strange, then US Open champion, was absolutely charming. He gave me an unhurried interview after his first round on the Thursday. I asked him again on the Friday and he dutifully stood alongside me for at least ten minutes until, unfortunately, events happening elsewhere dictated that I couldn't talk to him at all. Now, I know countless sportsmen who would have thrown a prima donna-type fit in such circumstances. Curtis didn't. He smiled and said that it wasn't a problem. I didn't see him again until the following year at Royal Troon. I'm sure he'd forgotten the incident almost the second it happened and he certainly wouldn't have had cause to remember who I was. Nevertheless, I reminded him and apologised profusely. He appreciated the gesture. A nice man. I always look for his scores and want him to do well . . . except when he played that singles match against Nick Faldo at Oak Hill in the Ryder Cup!

But back to Lytham, and I remember how thrilled I was to speak to golf's 'Big Three': Jack Nicklaus, Arnold Palmer and Gary Player. Player has public relations worked out to a fine art. He always finds out your first name before an interview begins. He knows it boosts the interviewer's ego and engenders an atmosphere of camaraderie if he responds to a question saying: 'Well, Alan . . .' implying that he's known you all your life. The other trademark of a Player interview is that he never has a bad word to say about the golf course. It's always 'one of the finest I've ever played'.

Palmer has an aura of greatness about him. I can barely remember 'Arnie's army'. I wasn't old enough. But, having been privileged enough to speak to him, I well understand how he inspired such loyalty and affection. And again, like so many golfers, particularly Americans, nothing was too much trouble. You got the impression that Palmer was simply that sort of person, though he'll have known the benefits to be accrued by being media friendly. If only footballers followed such examples.

I met Nicklaus in the clubhouse on the Saturday when play was washed out. Nicklaus is awesome. If you drew up a list of the outstanding sportsmen and women of the last century, he'd have to be on it and vying with the likes of Muhammad Ali for the top spot. I liked him instantly, though I also found his presence very intimidating. Beneath those soft looks of the all-American boy lurks an interior of the toughest steel. At the height of his career, Nicklaus must have frightened most of his opponents to death.

To be entirely accurate, it was Friday night's horrendous storm that did the damage, rendering the course unplayable for the following day. I walked through it with Gordon Turnbull, from our humble St Annes hotel to the rather plusher surroundings of the R & A headquarters. We were looking for the secretary, Michael Bonallack, who was able to tell us that, almost certainly, play would have to carry over to the Monday. We knew that would have repercussions for our coverage.

Renton Laidlaw was the presenter of our programmes. In media terms, he is 'Mr Golf'. Renton spends his entire life following the sport around the world and he reflects the gentility of the game. He's one of the nicest people you could wish to meet, with no 'side' to him. He is mild-mannered, delightfully witty, and nobody knows more about the game than he does. Clearly, I like him a great deal and rate him even more.

The problem, on the Monday, was that Renton's first responsibility was to the London *Evening Standard* for which he is golf correspondent. When we needed him on Radio 2, he had to be away filing copy for his paper. I was asked to fill the breach until Renton was free to come up to our box high above the eighteenth green. Only then could I be released to continue with my main role as interviewer. What an opportunity and how I loved it! Mind you, I was a little relieved when Renton finally arrived, with the closing moments approaching. My presentation skills were still primitive and I was straining to get to an area of broadcasting in which I felt much more comfortable.

Seve Ballesteros won his third Open Championship and I interviewed him live on the eighteenth green. Our conversation was also relayed over the public address system around the course. I was almost as pleased as Seve was.

On reflection, that must have been a fairly significant day in my career. Someone, again I don't know who, decided that in future I was to be a permanent member of the golf team, though not as a presenter/interviewer. By the 1989 Open, won by Mark Calcavecchia, I was roving the course, commentating on the action itself.

Open week is one of my favourite commitments each sporting year. The work is always physically draining. The radio commentators can be out on the course for the whole day, whatever the weather. I estimate that each of us walks between thirty-five and forty miles over the four days. Meal breaks? Forget about those. We're lucky to catch a sandwich. And you drink liquids at your peril. Play won't be held up just because you need to join a queue fifty deep for the toilet.

When we get back to our hotel about nine o'clock at night, having been at the course for at least twelve hours, we have barely enough energy to eat a meal before tumbling into bed. And when I say 'hotel', I use the term loosely. Open Championships aren't held in big cities where accommodation is plentiful and lavish. You're usually talking instead about remote Scottish towns where you're lucky to find a bed and breakfast, and if you've ever attended the Open you'll know what I mean. But let me tell you a little secret: before the R & A makes its annual announcement about where they'll be staging the championship four years hence, it informs people like the BBC. It's the only way the media can be guaranteed somewhere to stay.

I find the Open a very rewarding experience. I have been present to see some fantastic golf for over a decade. I've watched Faldo win two of his three titles, in 1990 and 1992. He would have won it again at Royal St George's in 1993 except for a brilliant final round 65 from Greg Norman. I was commentating on the Australian's progress every step of the way. I also stood barely twenty yards away describing John Daly's putt as it snaked a path into the second hole of his play-off against Costantino Rocca at St Andrews in 1995, virtually condemning the Italian to defeat. I followed every shot of Justin Leonard's final two rounds at Royal Troon two years later. His immaculate golf held off the challenge of Darren Clarke and Jesper Parnevik. It is such a privilege.

Yet I have to admit that for many years I didn't believe that golf commentary could work on the radio. It was, I thought, such a visual sport. How could you properly convey the images? Still, there's a phrase that you'll notice crops up fairly frequently in this book. 'I got it completely wrong.'

Television golf commentators tend to be isolated from the action. Their booth may be, for example, alongside the fourteenth fairway while what they're describing is happening on the sixth green. It means they can pitch their voices in a normal manner with no consideration of the effects on the golfers themselves or the spectators. Radio is totally different.

We walk the course, inside the ropes, and as close as we can get to the golfers without disturbing them. You creep along each hole, looking for vantage points. You may be crouched behind a bunker or alongside a tree. It's best to be downwind. Even a gentle breeze carries a whispered commentary a very long way and it's my experience that there isn't a golfer alive who can't hear a pin drop from fifty yards. Heaven help the radio commentator who's heard by a golfer addressing a putt. Thank goodness, it's only happened to me a couple of times. Seve once spun around with a piercing glare and I was saved only by my immediate and profuse apology. So, unless you're a long way from the green, you have to talk in whispers until the putt is struck and only then, in tandem with the crowd's response, can you give full vocal vent to what you're seeing. The commentary is hidden in the atmosphere.

Mind you, the television boys needn't be complacent. However distant they are from the shot they're describing, they can be tripped up by the multitude of monitors scattered throughout a course in hospitality booths. I remember Peter Alliss offering fulsome advice on how Greg Norman should play a difficult shot from a fairway bunker. Little did Alliss know that his commentary could be clearly heard by Norman from an unnecessarily loud monitor in a hospitality tent nearby. Norman backed off the shot, looked to some spectators and said: 'Perhaps he'd like to come out here and play it himself!'

On radio, we also need to take account of the spectators them-selves. Sometimes our best positions are also theirs, and since we're inside the ropes and they're outside, we might obscure their view. It can be impossible to avoid and for that I say sorry. Unfor-tunately, golf courses weren't designed for anybody other than golfers.

I suppose golf on radio can never replace the pictures on television, but it can transmit images that are just as appealing to those listening, even to those watching. It's an endearing tribute to *Test Match Special* that for many years a great deal of people have watched cricket on television with the mute button pressed and the radio on. It's happening, with increasing frequency, to football as well. And to golf.

It was a huge blow to BBC Television when they lost the rights to Sky Sports to broadcast the Ryder Cup live. I have to tell you, television's loss was BBC Radio's gain. There remains, however good their coverage, a public resistance to the influence of satellite television. As a consequence, Sky reaches far fewer people than it deserves to. At Oak Hill in 1995, our audience was estimated as at least three times that watching on satellite: over five million people were listening to golf on the radio!

It was an unmitigated triumph, 5 Live's coverage being rewarded with two Sony Golds, the radio equivalent of the Oscars. We were drowned in praise, particularly in the newspapers. This was Kate Battersby in the *Daily Telegraph*:

Sky Sports? Never heard of 'em. I watched the Ryder Cup on Radio 5 Live – and I do mean watched, as everyone else who did the same will understand . . .

One of the best aspects of 5 Live's twenty-two hours of coverage was the agreeably partisan tone: 'No offence, Ben,' whispered Alan Green as Crenshaw prepared to putt at the fifteenth in his match with Colin Montgomerie. 'But I don't mind if you miss this one.'

[The tone] was perfectly acceptable for two reasons. First, because anything excessive or distasteful, such as jingoism, was by definition out of the question. How can you be jingoistic about a pan-European team? And second, because the commentary team were not just scrupulous about applauding American play, but also clearly relished great golf whoever was playing it. But given that 5 Live coverage was for broadcast in Britain, there wasn't much doubt about whose side the listeners would be on. The commentators caught the mood.

'Are you listening, Nicholas?' asked George Bayley, sotto voce, as Faldo studied his putt at the seventeenth, the one he needed to win the hole and draw level with Curtis Strange. 'Get that putt in the hole. No nonsense now. I won't take no for an answer. Very simple now, Nicholas. This for the half, and I'll buy the drinks. He's over the ball. He's drawing the club back. The ball's on its way . . . AND IT'S IN THE HOLE!' Then Bayley, gripped with delirious mirth, concluded: 'Nick Faldo obviously listens to 5 Live.'

Faldo was not alone, judging by the drivers along London's Marylebone Road during the above piece of commentary. I was one of them. You know how you sometimes see a driver ahead of you bopping along to a song on the radio which you are also listening to? A group of cars had drawn up at a red traffic light as Bayley was promising to buy the drinks. I noticed several drivers around me leaning forward, their faces frozen, and as Faldo's putt dropped there was much clenching of fists and banging of steering wheels. Then we all realised that we were among many listening to the same station, we all laughed at each other.

In the end I had to pull over to listen to the closing moments. Otherwise I would have been in danger of causing a multiple pile-up.

Thank you, Kate.

★   ★   ★

Ah . . . the Ryder Cup! Clearly, it's difficult to argue against the status of football's World Cup as the greatest team competition in sport. The Olympic Games may be bigger but it has long been the preserve of the individual athlete in pursuit of personal gain as opposed to glory for the country he or she represents. So it's the World Cup, but the Ryder Cup comes close.

There is so much to love about it, not least how the intensity of its drama is matched by its purity. Of course, it would be naïve to think that there aren't massive financial spin-offs involved for those who take part. Think of how much more attractive a golfer is to sponsors having the label 'Ryder Cup' on his curriculum vitae. However, the fact remains that nobody, in either team, is paid to be there. Tiger Woods and Mark O'Meara, to their shame, complain about it, but you appear at Brookline or at the Belfry solely for the benefit of your colleagues, your country and your continent. Is that true anywhere else, in any sport?

As with the Open, my serious Ryder Cup involvement began in 1989. Two years previously, Europe had won for the first time on American soil, at Muirfield Village. Now it returned to the Belfry near Sutton Coldfield, where Tony Jacklin's captaincy had made its decisive breakthrough in 1985. I'd watched both matches on television and I couldn't wait to be part of it.

The American team flew in on Concorde to Birmingham Airport on the Sunday evening and I was among the thousands there to greet them. Most went there simply to cheer; I was one of a few who had to work. I was searching for US interviews and was aghast to discover how quickly the golfers were ushered through to their chauffeur-driven cars that would whisk them away to the Belfry Hotel. I was in a blind panic, thrusting a microphone at most everyone that I recognised, hoping for some words of comfort rather than insight. Most nodded politely and moved on. Freddie Couples, bless him, stopped and talked happily.

To me, there is no question that every reporter and commentator in sport finds his or her judgement affected, however marginally, by their perception of the person they are talking about. Some you like, some you can't stand. Unquestionably, Couples is one of the former. It's not simply that he follows the traditional American line of being helpful and respectful towards the media, Freddie is genuinely a great guy. Warm, charming, funny and intelligent. Mix in his good looks and his bank balance and it's no wonder he's massively popular with the opposite sex. I find he's one of those golfers that I always want to see doing well.

Unfortunately, for him and his team, Couples didn't have the best of Ryder Cups in 1989. He lost the only fourball in which he played and was beaten in the decisive singles match by Christy O'Connor Jnr. Consider it typical of Couples, though, that when O'Connor made the winning putt which provoked a tidal wave of European emotion, and Irish tears, it was greeted, too, by a firm handshake and a broad smile from the American. Like all the best sportsmen, Couples knows how to lose with style.

The United States should have lost the entire match. Europe, needing fourteen points to be certain of a tie and thereby certain of retaining the Cup, led 14–11 with three singles still being played out on the course. To this day, I feel guilty that I may have contributed somewhat to determining the final outcome.

Three points clear, with Gordon Brand Jnr, Nick Faldo and Ian Woosnam still playing, Europe required just a further half-point to win the Ryder Cup for the third successive time. Celebrations had, in truth, already begun. We awaited the half-point merely for confirmation.

I was sent to the sixteenth where Woosnam was lying one up on

Curtis Strange. As the buggy swung into the fairway, the Welshman stood waiting for the green to clear up ahead before playing his second shot. 'Woosie, have you heard?' I whispered. 'Europe have fourteen points. We can't lose.'

It may not have had any effect whatsoever. Only Ian could tell me. But perhaps the information I imparted took the edge off his play. He lost the last three holes to the US Open champion and the match. Faldo and Brand also lost. The Ryder Cup remained in Europe but overall it was a tie. You could sense just a tinge of disappointment.

How Europe would have rejoiced to achieve the same outcome two years later in South Carolina. Kiawah Island was a truly fantastic setting for the event. It is a magnificent course, reclaimed from swampland and bordered by the Atlantic Ocean. The organisers made sure everything was in perfect condition for the week. Though it most certainly was the wrong time of the year, whatever was sprayed before we arrived ensured that the usual plague of mosquitoes never materialised. Some of us were also concerned about the local population of alligators. Once again, the organisers took precautions. Any alligator over ten feet in length was temporarily 're-housed' and those that remained were so docile they must have been fed happy pills.

Now, as the last US captain Ben Crenshaw observed, the Ryder Cup is no place to have a picnic. Its intensity is relentless. Every single stroke matters and the spectators feel this just as much as the golfers. That's why, from the first tee shot on the Friday morning to the winning putt holed sometime on the Sunday afternoon, nobody escapes the tension and, of course, each side is desperate to win. However, in 1991, the importance of winning became far too important. Samuel Ryder would not have approved. His concept of highly competitive golf played in tandem with good manners and the highest standards of sporting behaviour was quickly lost in 'The War on the Shore'. Once play started, it became apparent, certainly on the American side, that only winning truly mattered and not how you won. It wasn't a pleasant experience. The US captain, Dave Stockton, so charged with American hurt at his country losing on the previous three occasions, shouldered most of the blame for the atmosphere, and deserved to. Unfortunately, he did get what he wanted, though only just.

Unlike every other Ryder Cup that I've attended, there wasn't a great deal of fun at Kiawah, but it had its moments. Naturally, covering the event as extensively as we do is a very expensive exercise, particularly when it's being staged in the United States. There isn't much money left over for frills. For example, we take only the essential number of engineers and they're required to manipulate and manage the sounds at 'base camp', somewhere near the clubhouse. We can't afford to have them out on the course carrying the equipment, as they would do at the Open. So we look for local volunteers, usually young golfers attached to the host club. They know the course, which is a great help to the commentator, and they find carrying the equipment a small price to pay for the privilege of watching such a great sporting event from inside the ropes. Usually.

On the Friday morning, a group of kids turned up, as appointed, to act as our 'back-packers'. Most didn't know what they were in for. I was delighted to find that the lad who was assigned to me was a single-handicap golfer himself and just loved the thought of doing anything that would allow him to see the Ryder Cup.

In contrast, Julian Tutt found himself saddled with a very different proposition. His young man didn't seem to like golf and certainly didn't appreciate the amount of energy expended on a normal Ryder Cup commentary shift. He soon tired of mirroring Julian's habit of pacing everything out so as to check the exact yardage of a shot. He ached for a rest. 'When do we break for lunch?' he inquired. 'Lunch?' said Julian. 'We don't get lunch. We'll have something to eat about six o'clock when play finishes.' It was about noon and this wasn't what the young man wanted to hear.

A short while later, he told Julian that he needed to go to the 'john'. Reluctantly, Julian granted him relief, put the radio pack on his own shoulders and asked the youngster to catch up with him further down the fairway. It was the last Julian saw of his back-packer, who left the course and never returned.

The BBC golf producer always has a plan of campaign to ensure that we have cover at every single hole where the event might be decided on the Sunday. Tony Adamson, the correspondent, rightly had the most privileged position. He was in our commentary box, which overlooked the eighteenth. Then, according to the scheme, each of the other commentators was assigned a singles match and told to take up residence at whichever hole that match finished, unless another commentator was already there. In that case, you either stopped at the hole before or walked through to the hole after, provided it, too, was unattended.

It sounds much more complicated than it actually is. Anyway, I was the lucky one. I went off that Sunday with the opening match, Nick Faldo against Raymond Floyd. For the sake of Europe, I'd have been happy for Faldo to win at any stage. However, selfishly, I didn't want him to close out his opponent until the eighteenth, with Tony able to describe the climax. That would leave me taking up station by the seventeenth green. If I couldn't commentate on the final hole, I knew that was the place to be.

Certain courses have signature holes, holes that are brought to mind throughout the world when particular venues are mentioned. The seventeenth at St Andrews, the 'Road Hole', is one of the best known, where a birdie three represents little short of a miracle. You think, too, of the tenth at the Belfry, a relatively easy par four that nevertheless offers the possibility of an eagle two to the boldest player. The seventeenth at Kiawah ranks in the same league.

It's a short hole but the shot from tee to green has to negotiate a lake. There is no 'get-out'. Hackers such as myself would rather die than play it, yet even the world's finest golfers find themselves unnerved by the challenge. Ball after ball found that lake on the first two days and the Sunday there provided some of the most dramatic action that I've ever seen on a golf course. It was where David Feherty won his match against Payne Stewart and could hardly stop talking in his pleasure before dissolving in tears.

It was there that Mark Calcavecchia drove into the water, then watched his opponent, Colin Montgomerie, do exactly the same. Up stepped Mark for his second attempt. Again the ball found the water. Montgomerie, having previously been four down with four to play, took the hole and, soon afterwards, a half-point from a match he looked certain to lose. Calcavecchia was devastated, inconsolable.

It was there, too, that Corey Pavin, war-maker in chief on the US team with his 'Desert Storm' cap, went on a victory parade, circling the green time after time, after his defeat of Steven Richardson. Where Chip Beck made sure of beating Ian Woosnam and Paul Broadhurst defeated Mark O'Meara. All of this happened on the seventeenth green.

It seemed fated that the destiny of the 1991 Ryder Cup would also be decided on the seventeenth green, though I hoped that it wouldn't. When Bernhard Langer and Hale Irwin stood on the tee, every other member of the two teams was around the putting surface. Everyone knew that unless Langer won the hole and took the match to the eighteenth, the United States would regain the trophy. I didn't want that outcome. I erupted in as much joy as the whole European team when Langer stroked in the key putt. Ballesteros and Olazabal jumped up alongside me, and while I continued to describe the fantastic scenes around me, they rushed off with the others to the next tee. I knew immediately that I'd never make it.

Every spectator on the course was scrambling for a vantage point on the final hole. It was impossible. I ran down the side of the fairway, hoping that the sighs and roars would keep me informed of what was going on. Finally, I dashed into the press tent and slumped exhausted by the video screen.

If Langer holed another putt, the match would finish as it had done at the Belfry in 1989, as a tie, and Europe would retain the Ryder Cup. Nobody should be asked to hole a putt of such significance, a point made vociferously by Ballesteros afterwards. Nobody should be expected to hole such a putt. Langer missed.

I trudged back to our centre of operations, as depressed as could be. I wasn't consoled by the fantastic nature of the climax. That was a thought best left for the future. When I climbed into the van, half the BBC team was in tears. You see, the Ryder Cup gets to you like no other sports event.

The 1993 competition, back at the Belfry, to a degree continued the European depression that had set in at Kiawah. The Americans held sway again though Europe squandered chances to win on the final day. It felt a little as if that traditional air of American superiority had settled over the Ryder Cup once more.

Oak Hill quickly dismissed such thinking and I suppose what made it so special was that it was so unexpected. Europe trailed 9–7 after the first two days. Corey Pavin and Loren Roberts were paraded before the media in triumphal fashion after they'd won what seemed a crucial final Saturday afternoon fourball against Faldo and Langer. Almost everyone, and certainly the US team, went to bed that night believing a home victory was now assured. The Americans were usually so much stronger in the singles. Only the European captain, Bernard Gallacher, begged to differ. I interviewed him in the clubhouse well after sunset and he spoke confidently about the line-ups for the following day. I thought it merely brave talk.

And that's how it seemed in the early stages of the final day. You can gauge how any Ryder Cup is going by a swift glance at the scoreboards that proliferate around the course. How does the blue relate to the red? Too much red tells you that the Americans are in control. That's how it was, the colour confirming my own expectations.

I can't tell you precisely when it happened but I know where I was when fortunes began to shift. I was beside the green on the short fifteenth. Looking at the scoreboard, across the putting surface, and doing my mental arithmetic, I suddenly thought: 'Hey. Europe can win this. But Sam Torrance has to hold on against Roberts, Philip Walton needs to beat Jay Haas and even then, Faldo needs to stage a comeback against Curtis Strange.' It was unlikely but it was possible.

I was watching Torrance tee off at the fifteenth when I felt a firm, urgent tap on my shoulder. It was Seve. Ballesteros had played the opening singles against Tom Lehman and had been well beaten 4 and 3. Now he was acting as cheerleader for his colleagues.

'Diz putt of Nick's. How long?' Nick Faldo had been in trouble on the sixteenth and needed to make a vital putt. If he lost the hole Strange would lie 'dormie two' and the Americans would be certain of the half-point they needed to retain the Cup. 'How long, Seve? I don't know. I'll ask.'

I contacted the producer, Rob Nothman. 'Rob, Seve's with me. He wants to know how long Faldo's putt is on sixteen.' Eight feet, came the reply. Seve was hyperventilating. 'Iz difficult? He make it?' How the hell would I know? I took off my headphones and put them on Seve. I waited for the response, which would tell me whether or not the putt was holed. The Spaniard yelled in delight, threw off the headset, smiled his thanks to me and ran off behind the fifteenth green seeking the seventeenth fairway to await Faldo. It was a fantastic moment.

A while later, at the same spot, watching the final singles between Per-Ulrik Johanssen and Phil Mickelson, there was another tap on my shoulder. A polite one this time. It was the Duke of York. Now, Prince Andrew is a golf fanatic, present at every Open and every Ryder Cup. Many times I've asked him for an interview. Every time, he thanks me and politely declines the request. Once, somewhat obscurely, he offered the explanation: 'I'm not sure the Palace would approve.'

He asked how Faldo was doing. Faldo was by now on the final hole, needing to win it. He'd played a magnificent wedge shot from ninety-three yards to leave himself with a four-foot putt. There wasn't anyone on the golf course who didn't realise the significance of that putt.

Mickelson and Johanssen were also on the green. I had to be careful. While the American was lining up his putt, I was relaying in whispers to the Duke what was happening to Faldo. The putts were almost simultaneous. Mickelson missed. Faldo holed. Prince Andrew squealed in delight. Mickelson must have thought it was in relation to his putt, but it's one thing ticking off an errant commentator. It's quite another when royalty is involved.

Suddenly, I realised that I might be commentating again. I dashed across to the eighteenth, all the while listening to what Walton was doing on the seventeenth. If he halved the hole then the Ryder Cup was Europe's again. I was among thousands lining the final fairway.

Actually, I was pacing it, adrenaline surging through me as if I was playing and not merely commentating. Haas won seventeen.

Up ahead, Tony Adamson was with Tommy Horton in the commentary box behind the green. Julian Tutt was down the right-hand side of the fairway; I was down the left. The American was first to tee off. The absence of 'You're the man' and 'Way to go' quickly told me that Haas had faltered. The drive was heading in my direction but wasn't even that good. Tony and Tommy were speculating about the trouble the ball might be in. I could see it. 'It's right behind a huge oak tree. He doesn't have a shot to play other than sideways!'

Walton was next, with the advantage. But he, too, erred. Down the right this time, into the thick rough. As I had been for Haas's drive, Julian was perfectly placed to say what had happened.

Tony and Tommy still had their doubts. Horton was speculating about how Haas might find a way around and through the trees. I knew that no such option existed. Mark James, who'd won 4 and 3 against Jeff Maggert, came alongside me. He delivered the definitive verdict on the American's position. 'He hasn't a shot except to play it sideways on to the fairway and hope for a good third on to the green.'

Up came Ian Woosnam. 'Have you seen Phil's ball, Ian?' I asked.

'Yeah, he's fine. The ball's sitting up nicely. He can get a four or five wood to it.' Both told me how relieved they were to be watching rather than playing at this moment. The pressure was too great. 'I'm off up to the green,' said Woosie. 'This is getting too much.' James, the future captain, stayed with me.

Haas made the green with his third shot but was in two-putt territory. Walton's second lay in the rough at the bottom of the slope in front of the putting surface. James pronounced that he was 'in good nick'.

By this time I, too, was by the green, crawling among the European team to get into the best position. I accidentally knelt on someone's foot. I looked up. It was the Duke of York. 'Sorry, Sir!' I literally clambered over Faldo and his caddy, Fanny Suneson. My target was

Seve. After the fifteenth, I knew, and he knew, that he owed me some words.

Walton was about to play his third shot. I thrust the microphone towards Ballesteros. I can't remember now what he said but each and every listener got the message. Walton was safely on the green. 'Will he do it, Seve?' 'Iz fifteen feet! Iz two putts! He can do it! He can do it!' Walton did it.

When he lagged the first putt up close to the hole, Haas conceded. Immediately, the eighteenth green was engulfed in the celebrations of the European team. Julian and I were in among them. Naturally, Gallacher was first to Walton, lifting the Irishman high off his feet. I got to the captain almost as quickly. He could hardly speak for joy: 'We just won it! We won it! We won it!' Seve chipped in with further incisive analysis: 'Iz funtustic! Iz grite! Iz onbellevabul!' That's it. 'Iz' the Ryder Cup.

I was so looking forward to Brookline. The Country Club is situated no more than fifteen minutes' drive from the centre of one of my favourite American cities, Boston. A wonderful course in one of the best areas of the United States. Who could ask for more?

Everything I'd heard about the venue was confirmed by my first views of it. It felt so English you thought you were at Wentworth: the rolling, unusually wide fairways; the abundance of trees. I immediately sensed that even if it didn't actually give the European team an advantage, it certainly wouldn't hamper them.

I only wish that I'd felt so confident about what we were out there for. The PGA of America, for whom BBC 5 Live was providing on-course commentary (the little receivers, which cost $12, were among the hottest-selling items in the Ryder Cup Village), refused to give us the tools of the trade. Our access was restricted to going no further than three feet inside the ropes. Protests that we couldn't properly provide our normal service were brushed aside.

Each morning, we left our hotel in downtown Boston at 5.30 a.m. in order to reach the course in time to start broadcasting when the first tee shot was played two hours later. There was just room to squeeze in a little breakfast. I remember that Friday morning suggesting that we hold a sweep, $5 a head, on what the score would be at the end of the first foursomes and fourballs. Being a natural pessimist, I forecast a 6–2 lead for the United States. All bar one of the thirteen participants also went for an American lead. Paul Eales, the European tour professional and one of our summarisers, said it would be 6–2 to Europe. He was ridiculed, some suggested a suitable case for the funny farm. Paul soon had $65 extra in his pocket.

I sat with him on the coach back to the hotel that night. 'How could it have happened?' I asked.

'It's straightforward,' he said. 'Everyone underestimates our golfers and exaggerates the ability of the Americans. The world rankings are a load of tosh.'

The golf had been incredible, from both sides. During the afternoon, Davis Love III had had to hole an eagle putt at the fourteenth simply to halve the hole! At the sixteenth, I paused to reflect on what we were witnessing. 'Isn't the Ryder Cup just wonderful? Wouldn't it be great if you could bottle it and then, on those occasional nights when you're feeling lonely or depressed, you could open it up and have a sip.' People around me, listening on their special radios, started to laugh in agreement. As I left the hole one shouted after me: 'I'll have a six-pack of this Ryder Cup stuff!'

Come the Saturday night, Europe still held a four-point lead. Surely it would be their third Ryder Cup win in succession. All logic pointed to that outcome. But that's it, isn't it? How can you predict what will happen in any Ryder Cup? The event has become impossible to call. That Europe should have won is irrelevant. The Americans holed their putts and blew the Europeans away. Collectively, in this singles, they were 38 under par to Europe's 10 under. Simply, they played the better golf, astounding golf.

And – this isn't written in hindsight – once I'd seen how the singles matches lined up, I had a bad feeling. It was surely expecting too much of Jarmo Sandelin, Jean Van de Velde and Andrew Coltart to have sat out all the foursome and fourball matches and then win points against Phil Mickelson, Davis Love and Tiger Woods. It was the one area in which Mark James couldn't escape criticism. If he had so little faith in Coltart, why did he pick him? Far better, surely, to have had the experience of a Bernhard Langer on board. Europe ended up needing all their big guns to deliver and, not surprisingly, they couldn't keep on delivering.

Unfortunately, the fact that the United States definitely deserved to win was largely forgotten in the aftermath. It's true that some of the spectators behaved disgracefully. At the twelfth, a woman who must have been in her sixties hollered in delight when a European ball scurried into a bunker. I scolded her as I would have done a naughty child. 'Don't do that. Cheer your own team on but don't abuse their opponents.' She dismissed the criticism. I went further. 'If you were European, and you said that at the Belfry, I'd be ashamed. You should be ashamed of yourself.' She took the hint and shut up. I wish more of her fellow countrymen and women had done the same. And the rabble-rousing by many of the US golfers didn't help either.

I wasn't at the seventeenth green when Justin Leonard holed the incredible putt that provoked those outrageous scenes of celebration. I only saw the incident later on television. Of course, they were wrong. That should not have happened, particularly on the sacred surface that is the putting green. But, let's say Sergio had holed a putt to win the Ryder Cup for Europe, would the reaction of our golfers have been any less? Sadly, I doubt it.

Some of the European response was as over the top as the Americans had been. Mark James, as upset by the defeat as by the treatment, said he wouldn't play in the United States again. His deputy, Sam Torrance, was apoplectic with rage. No doubt it was heartfelt, but that will be remembered, by friend and foe, and won't help lower the temperature for 2001 when the Ryder Cup returns to the Belfry, when Torrance is captain. I can see a lot of 'football fans' wanting to join in any abuse aimed at the Americans.

Yet, something so sad that happened afterwards may leave a better legacy than a few bitter memories of Brookline. Precisely a month later, I was in Italy waiting for Chelsea's Champions League fixture against AC Milan. My wife told me in a phone call that Payne Stewart had died in a plane crash.

There haven't been many bigger patriots than Payne. In Ryder Cups, he liked to wrap himself up in the Stars and Stripes as the critical moments were reached. Yet his respect for the sport, his colleagues and his opponents, was immense. Payne never tolerated any bad behaviour. He berated those who threw insults at Colin Montgomerie when they played against each other during the Sunday singles. 'That's enough,' he said. 'That's EEEE-NOUGH!'

The two reached the eighteenth green with Montgomerie one up and having two putts to win. Stewart conceded the hole. It meant a win for the Scot and defeat for Stewart. He didn't care. 'I wasn't going to make him hole that. He didn't deserve to have to. My personal stats don't mean crap.'

Payne Stewart was a gentleman of golf and the sport misses him terribly. He embodied what the Ryder Cup is all about. He had a great talent, was a fierce competitor, but he always knew how to behave. Anyone plotting revenge at the Belfry, in any other terms but golfing, should remember Payne Stewart and think again.

CHAPTER THIRTEEN

THE GREEN BAIZE

W hen I first joined BBC Radio Sport in 1982, I'm not sure that they quite knew what to do with me. 'Slim' Wilkinson, who was head of department, certainly wanted to have me on his staff. However, with me isolated in the north of England, it was always likely that both of us would need a bedding-in period finding out, from his point of view, what I'd be best at and, from mine, what I'd most enjoy. Neither of us properly knew what was ahead.

Initially, I seemed to spend a lot of my time watching games at Highfield Road. I mean no offence to Coventry City, but that was not what I had in mind in becoming Radio Sport's representative in the north of England. It didn't take me long to point out the absurdity of the situation and within months, I finally got to learn how to get to Anfield and Old Trafford.

There was also the question of finding out which sports, other than football, I could work on. Making features for programmes such as *Sport on 4* soon had me involved in activities as diverse as hang-gliding, long-distance swimming, even (the mind still boggles) ferret racing! I'll never forget how, without any conviction whatsoever, I went to an obscure Yorkshire village to watch this 'sport' in action.

Thankfully, I had an audio engineer with me who kept a straight enough face to record what went on. I thought the whole business was a complete farce and totally inappropriate to be broadcast on Radio 4. Not for the last time, I was completely wrong. 'Ferret Racing' turned out to be one of the better features I made for the programme, presented then so ably by Cliff Morgan.

Football remained at the centre of my early work for the department but I welcomed the variety of other sport that I was invited to cover and in April 1982, I was asked to report on the Embassy World Professional Snooker Championship at the Crucible Theatre in Sheffield.

I'd had some involvement in the sport in Northern Ireland. Alex Higgins, world champion in 1972, and Dennis Taylor, who'd been runner-up to Terry Griffiths in 1979, were among the primary sporting celebrities in the province. Naturally, they were top interview targets when they returned home and because of that, I already knew both of them, though Dennis rather better than Alex. It helped. They were friendly faces to look out for in my first encounter with the Crucible.

I think it is one of the great sporting venues. Believe me, the intense drama relayed by the television cameras is as nothing to the experience of being there. Nearly twenty years on from first seeing it, I still marvel at the intimacy of the arena. It accommodates barely 900 people so there is nowhere to hide. You're frightened to cough, never mind talk. You feel more than slightly claustrophobic. And pity the person in desperate need of a visit to the lavatory. Except at the end of a break, you simply can't go.

Nowadays, the seventeen days of the championship begin on a Saturday but in 1982, it opened on a Friday evening. As always, the defending champion started proceedings. The previous year, Steve Davis had been one of the many sporting superstars whom I knew only from a television screen. Now, I was watching him in action only a few feet away, hardly daring to breathe for fear of disturbing him. Whatever, there was nothing I did that Friday night to provoke the awful situation Davis found himself in at the end of the first session. He trailed Tony Knowles by eight frames to one, only two frames away from a wholly unexpected first-round defeat. This was big news.

Without asking, I was aware *Sport on 4* would relish the opportunity to hear from the world champion. It was very unusual then, and still is now, to conduct any interview mid-match, but I had to try. I walked out of the press room and along the short corridor to the dressing rooms. Timidly, I knocked on Davis's door.

His manager, Barry Hearn, opened it. I introduced myself and asked to talk to Steve. Hearn stood to one side allowing me to see into the room. 'I'm sorry,' he said, 'look at him.' Davis was leaning against the sink, head bowed, deep in thought. 'He's wrecked. He can't talk to anybody at the moment.'

I understood, but I had to press the point. 'Believe me, I wouldn't ask normally, but he *is* the world champion.'

'Sorry, I can't help. I promise you this. Win or lose tomorrow morning, I'll bring Steve to you to be interviewed.'

The door closed and I walked back down towards the press room. I was disappointed but not surprised. How would anyone feel, never mind a world champion, when they're on the end of an embarrassing thrashing?

I hurried to the broadcast point to tell London that I had tried and failed. However, before I had time to lift the telephone, Hearn appeared at my side. 'He's coming now. Steve will talk to you tonight.' Now, perhaps it wasn't the greatest interview you'll ever hear. Davis was truly shattered, as you'd expect. But he did respond to all my questions, including the naïve ones.

Steve made such an impression on me that night. That, I thought, is how a true champion conducts himself, and he's never changed. Don't believe that nonsense tag of him being 'boring'. Even as a very young man, carrying the burden of fame and fortune, Steve was approachable, humorous and highly articulate. He also 'remembers'. I met him again, years after I'd stopped reporting on the sport and it was as if it had only been yesterday. He still teased me about my accent and about my involvement with football.

Davis lost to Knowles on the Saturday morning and again he didn't duck the media. That strength of character, as well as his supreme ability, helped him win the world championship six times. I was lucky to be present at all but this first victory.

But 1982 was the year of Alex Higgins, the self-styled 'people's champion'. It's harsh on Steve Davis and Stephen Hendry, both of them significantly better players, but only Jimmy White approached Higgins in terms of popularity with the public. The fans loved the Irishman for so passionately wearing his heart on his sleeve. They adored his style around the table. How he never wore a tie or a dicky-bow because of some seemingly spurious medical dispensation and how he left the top shirt button undone. How he paced edgily between shots. But above all, they worshipped his ability with a cue. No one who was there will forget the clearance Higgins made to defeat White in the semi-final. There was no margin for error. It may have been barely half the total of inspired and televised 147s but that 69 break was the greatest I've ever seen.

Exhilarated though Higgins was to win, he was genuinely distraught that White was the loser. Alex loves Jimmy. He has always seen in the Londoner a younger version of himself. I'm sure, given the chance, Alex would happily transfer to Jimmy either of his two world titles. If millions of followers are sorry that White never became world champion, I believe Higgins feels the hurt most of all.

Both were wonderful to watch. Their matches flew by with dazzling speed. Yet, generally, as far as the media is concerned, the working day at the Crucible can be very long, a point really brought home to me the second year I covered the world championship. Though he didn't win the title, Steve Davis regaining his crown by beating him in the final, Cliff Thorburn dominated the 1983 event.

The Canadian was a marvellous character. He'd emerged from the professional pool circuit in North America and taken the world snooker title in 1980. He was playing well enough to suggest he'd win again three years later. In the quarter-finals, against Terry Griffiths, Thorburn scored the first ever Crucible 147. Even Griffiths was cheering.

Now, neither of them was exactly quick around the table – precisely the opposite of a White or a Higgins. Their final session was due to be completed that evening. In fact, it stumbled into the early hours of the following morning.

BBC television cameras were switched off shortly after 1 a.m. Union rules prevented them from continuing to record the match. Live coverage had already ended long before. Gradually, too, spectators began to drift away. The snooker was engrossing but very slow. With the heat of the Crucible, some fans had fallen asleep.

I couldn't. I still had reports to file for the morning and I couldn't do them until the match finished. When it did – at 3.53 a.m. – there were barely a hundred people left watching, three of them journalists: Steve Acteson of the Press Association, Clive Everton, the leading BBC television commentator and editor of *Snooker Scene*, and myself. Each of us had been working at the Crucible since 9.30 the previous morning.

Can you believe that both players agreed to hold a press conference at half-past four? An hour later, I was still reading Steve's copy and he was listening to my intended reports to make sure that neither of us had gone completely gaga!

I remember walking back to the Grosvenor House Hotel as dawn broke over Sheffield. I got into my bed around half-past six, setting the alarm for two hours later. I had to start working again at half-past nine.

For much of the following day, I walked around the venue like a zombie. I might have been tempted into suicide had anyone told me in advance that I'd still be there at 1.30 a.m. for the conclusion of Thorburn's match against his fellow Canadian, Kirk Stevens. I'd had two hours' sleep, and worked the rest, in a period of forty hours. Don't believe anyone who tells you my life is all glamour! Yet I wouldn't have changed a thing in those astonishing couple of days. The adrenaline easily kept me going. I was privileged to watch some of the finest snooker ever played. How could anyone complain?

I've always felt the eighties represented the true golden era of the sport. They were great players and, just as important, they were great characters. Whatever the sport, it's wrong and it's too easy for participants and observers to say that it was all better in their day. I never got to know Hendry as well as I knew Davis and I certainly believe that Ronnie O'Sullivan is as exciting a player as we've ever seen. But, partly because I stopped covering the sport in a professional sense, the nineties didn't leave me as spellbound as the previous decade. I'm probably just getting old and grumpy.

Let me tell you, though, one further snooker story that emphasises to me how much I owe the sport. You've read elsewhere about Hillsborough. That FA Cup semi-final will stain my memory forever and I clearly remember most everything associated with that day.

As I've described, the game clashed with the opening frames of the

Gathering my thoughts during an *Arena* documentary on commentary. (*BBC*)

Sometimes sportsmen can surprise you by their consideration for others. I will never forget how Tony Knowles helped me after I had witnessed the horrors of Hillsborough. (*Colorsport*)

It's a tough life: working at the Benson & Hedges Open Tournament. (*Hailey Sports Photographic*)

The tension mounts during the 1995 Ryder Cup at Oak Hill. Tommy Horton stands alongside me while behind him HRH Prince Andrew gets as close to the action as possible. (*Hailey Sports Photographic*)

Nick Faldo's superb third shot on the 18th sets up victory for Europe in the 1995 Ryder Cup. (*David Cannon/Allsport*)

The funny thing is I get paid to enjoy myself. (*Actionimages*)

Possibly the greatest British sportsman of all time: Steve Redgrave slumps in his boat after winning a fourth consecutive gold medal in the 1996 Olympic games. Matthew Pinsent is his partner. It was perhaps the most dramatic and emotional sporting moment in my commentating career. (*Ross Kinnaird/Allsport*)

1989 World Snooker Championship. Football had to be my priority and the plan was for me to commentate at Hillsborough and then move to the Crucible for the Saturday evening session and every one thereafter.

I was in automatic as I drove to the venue, first dropping off Peter Jones at the railway station, both of us in tears. It was around 6.30 p.m. I somehow managed to stem those tears as I picked up my accreditation at the stage door. In a daze, I walked along the familiar corridor, past the dressing-rooms, the press canteen, towards the press room itself. Within a couple of yards of the entrance, I bumped into Steve Acteson. He didn't say anything. He looked into my eyes. Everyone there knew what had happened and they were anxiously awaiting my arrival, not knowing what to expect. Steve was, and remains, a very good friend. I broke down, collapsing into his arms. He dragged me into the gents' toilets where I sobbed uncontrollably. In came Tony Knowles.

Now Knowles, who's from Bolton, had a bit of a reputation. In terms of his snooker, he certainly worked hard, but he also knew how to play hard. He liked a drink, he liked to go clubbing, and his boyish film-star looks acted like a magnet to women. Famously, he once posed semi-naked across a snooker table for a tabloid newspaper. He was seen as a bit of a wild boy.

He was about to play his first-round match and though he'd heard of the tragedy at Hillsborough, he didn't know that I'd been there. Steve told him, and Tony forgot about his match. He was only concerned for my welfare.

That evening, I was comforted by the support of colleagues who were also good friends, people like Steve, Clive and Janice Hale. I got seriously drunk. It dulled the senses but not the memory.

I decided on the Sunday that I needed to stay on at the snooker to help take my mind off what I'd witnessed. I can't say that I actually watched a single frame that day but I got through my reporting commitments.

Knowles finished his match. He lost and, unless there's a specific request otherwise, only winning players are expected to face the media afterwards. Tony was well beaten, and must have wished for the comfort of Bolton. Yet he came to the press room to seek me out. How was I? We talked for a few minutes and it was a gesture that I will never forget. It was typical of the snooker scene that I loved and still miss.

CHAPTER FOURTEEN

MESSING ABOUT ON THE RIVER

A ugust 31 1997 is a day that is certain to be long remembered. In the early hours of that Sunday morning Diana, Princess of Wales, was tragically killed in an accident as her chauffeur-driven Mercedes sped through the streets of Paris. A world, as well as a nation, mourned.

I heard the news in what would otherwise have been somewhat farcical circumstances. The previous afternoon, I had flown to Lyon in the Savoy region of France for the World Rowing Championships. They were being staged on Lac Aiguebelette, a beautiful setting in the foothills of the Alps, about an hour and a half's drive away. Unfortunately, British Airways had neglected to send my luggage with me.

I woke up early in my hotel room in Aix-les-Bains, determined to telephone the lost-luggage office at Heathrow the very second it was due to open at 8 a.m. 'What's going on?' I inquired. 'I can understand the bags missing my flight, it can happen . . . but why didn't they make the next one? Never mind that I haven't got a clean shirt or a fresh pair of socks, all my technical equipment is missing. I won't be able to broadcast. The BBC won't be very happy.'

'I shouldn't worry,' the attendant replied, 'I don't think your colleagues will be that interested in the rowing today.'

'What do you mean?'

'Oh, you haven't heard the news?' And, no, I hadn't heard the news.

Though I was to be isolated from the outpouring of grief that engulfed the United Kingdom over the following days, it was immediately obvious that the planned coverage of the championships simply wouldn't happen. More important matters took precedence. There was nothing else to do but spend the week renewing old friendships that had first been established the previous year during the Olympic Games.

This was something of a worry for me. I hadn't been involved in any rowing whatsoever since Atlanta. Why should anyone remember me? Did I have to start again?

This was the thought in my head as, arriving at the venue, I walked down towards one of the boat docks. Greg Searle, who had won a gold medal in the coxed pair with his brother Johnny in the Barcelona Olympics, had now switched to the single sculls event. He'd just competed successfully in the opening heat and I wanted to say: 'Hi, well done, you won't remember me, I'm Alan Green from BBC 5 Live . . .' I should have known. Before I got within thirty yards of Greg, there was a big friendly wave to match his smile: 'Greenie, where have you been? We've missed you. Welcome back.' His reaction was completely typical of how the rowing community had embraced me as one of their own. This for someone who had never been in a boat and still can't swim.

Truth be told, I never expected to have any relationship with rowing.

It was in August 1995, sitting in the office of the Head of Radio Sport discussing the world and his wife, that Bob Shennan suddenly brought up the subject of the Olympics. He explained that he was keen to get me on board the team to go to Atlanta but, obviously, football wasn't going to form anything other than a minor part of radio's coverage. 'Alan, what do you know about rowing?' I told him that I knew as much about rowing as he thought I knew – nothing! 'How would you fancy commentating on rowing next summer? Steve Redgrave and Matthew Pinsent are one of Britain's main hopes for a gold medal. We're aiming to give the sport a lot of airtime. I'd like you to take it on.'

Bluntly, if he had suggested tiddlywinks as a means of my getting to the Olympics, I would probably have said yes, but I've never taken on anything that I wasn't reasonably confident of and I wasn't at all sure about rowing. I wanted to be certain that I would be able to overcome my almost total lack of knowledge. I didn't want to embarrass either the sport or myself. So, I asked Bob for time to think about it. I needed to make a few calls.

The first was to Dan Topolski, the former coach of the Oxford Boat Race crew. Dan was an essential ingredient of BBC Television's coverage, someone who had forgotten more about the sport than I would ever learn. I went to meet him at his London home and I freely admit I found the experience daunting. After all, this was a sport I knew next to nothing about and I admitted this to him. In a way, I was asking Dan if he felt it was possible for me to learn enough, quickly enough, so that I wouldn't make a complete ass of myself. Instead, it was as if it was the other way round. I sensed that he was trying to sell the sport to me. It wasn't difficult, partly because I was immediately inspired by his enthusiasm.

Next, I arranged to meet Redgrave and Pinsent along with their coach, Jurgen Grobler. I had already come across Matt when he had been a guest on my *Sportstalk* programme on 5 Live. You couldn't fail to be impressed by his intelligence and his pronounced sense of humour. I knew everything would be fine with him. However, I wasn't so sure of the other two.

Steve is wary of people he doesn't know and I had been warned as much. So I wasn't surprised that morning at Henley, sharing a late breakfast of bacon butties and orange juice at Leander Rowing Club, that Redgrave sat very quietly in the corner. Indeed, Grobler, who had been one of the leading coaches in the old East German regime, was a pussycat in comparison. Despite the language barrier (mine not his) we quickly got on well together.

As the chat continued, I became increasingly concerned that I didn't seem to be hitting it off with Steve, no matter that Matt had already told him that I was okay. I don't know how it happened – perhaps it was my probing about how they relaxed away from their incredibly strenuous training programme – but somehow the subject of golf came up. I could see the sparkle in Steve's eyes when he discovered that I also commentated on golf. A few anecdotes later and we were laughing and joking. The surface ice had been broken and I left Henley in a much happier frame of mind than when I'd arrived.

Of course, I still knew little about rowing. I spent the remaining winter months reading as much as I could, though you'd be surprised at how little there was to read. I found it more helpful studying videos of the previous world championships in Tampere, Finland. Despite the appalling weather, the racing was magnificent and I was particularly taken by the final of the single sculls, won by the great Slovenian, Iztok Cop. I was enthralled. For the first time I knew that this was a sport I could respond to.

In May, I stepped off a flight from Hong Kong, where England had been preparing for Euro 96, and immediately boarded a plane for Zurich. I was en route to Lucerne for the biggest regatta of the year outside of Atlanta. The travel left me exhausted and not best able to approach members of the British squad who knew even less about me than I did about them. My hotel was a short walk away from theirs.

I asked for David Tanner, the British team manager. I didn't even know what David looked like but the calm, softly spoken figure that appeared in front of me fitted easily with his regular employment as a school headmaster. The exterior disguised a passionate devotee of rowing who is as single-minded in his pursuit of winning races as he is determined that the sport should receive due public recognition. It was clear from our first introduction that we had much in common.

You can just imagine Glenn Hoddle or Kevin Keegan inviting me to share lunch, at their expense, with the England football team. Yet that is precisely the equivalent of what David did to this total stranger. 'Have you eaten? No? Come and have lunch. I'll introduce you to everyone.' And he did. Again, I was left to wonder just who was courting whom.

The following morning, the day before the start of the regatta on the Rotsee, was to be just as important. Martin Cross was due to arrive at my hotel. He was to be my expert summariser during the Olympics. I'd heard a lot about Martin as well as knowing about his rowing pedigree. He'd won an Olympic gold medal in the same boat as Redgrave at Los Angeles in 1984 and their paths had crossed in other ways too. Martin had been engaged to Anne, the British team doctor, who later became Steve's wife. For a time, they'd been rivals in love as well as in rowing, and while Steve was generally quiet, Martin was positively effervescent. They rightly say you need a good mix in any successful boat.

The easiest way to express how well Martin and I got on is to tell you that we were certain of becoming pals for life by the end of our first meal together. Perhaps the three bottles of excellent red wine that we shared had something to do with it, but we both knew this was merely the gelling of two like-minded personalities. It was obvious to each other that we'd become a great team.

Yet the regatta itself didn't ease any lingering concerns. We were meant to be doing some trial commentary and I immediately encountered problems. The racing, remember, is over a 2,000 metre course. The boats are literally dots in the distance when the klaxon sounds. Until they come within 300 metres, the commentator is totally reliant on a television monitor to follow what's going on. So he is dependent on the ability of the television director to offer up pictures that tell the story of the race. Unfortunately, not all of them are up to it.

This particular director was more interested in big close-ups than the bigger picture, either showing faces grimacing in pain or faces that were simply 'pretty'. Frequently, he concentrated on one boat, and you hadn't a clue whether it was in front, trailing or merely contained the greatest proportion of attractive bodies.

Worse, a lack of foresight in the London office meant that Martin and I had been booked a commentary position on the press side of the lake, opposite where the television commentators sat. With the naked eye, the boats were travelling from right to left, whereas the television monitor showed them moving left to right. I was confused enough without that hindrance. I flew home on the Sunday evening delighted with the relationships that I had formed but as bewildered as ever about my ability to do the job properly. It was too late now, though, to change my mind.

Not many of the BBC team enjoyed the Atlanta experience. They were ensconced in a grubby hotel on the edge of an unattractive city. The transport system installed to take competitors and media to and from the venues was an absolute joke. Drivers had been brought in from out of state and they knew the roads no better than their passengers did. Some buses got lost, most were late, and a few never arrived. It was chaos. Boy, was I glad to be out of it!

Lake Lanier is nearly seventy miles out of Atlanta and was a wonderful venue with its beautiful scenery and its warm, friendly people. Whatever my colleagues were suffering elsewhere, I knew that I was in the right place. Yet it too had transportation problems. The morning I arrived, I discovered I would need to catch four different buses to get from my motel to the commentary positions. Never known for my shyness, I told the BBC chief in Atlanta that he could forget that. He'd have to get me a car. And he did.

That Olympic regatta was one of the most enjoyable working experiences of my life. Actually, to call it 'work' is to mislead. It was fun from beginning to end. The work was easy. I was made to feel that I was part of the British squad; no interview request was too much trouble. I had David Tanner's mobile number but I hardly needed to use it. Each morning, within minutes of sitting down at my position, well before the start of racing, my phone would ring, and it would be David. Who did I want to talk to today? When? Where? It would be done. There could not be a greater contrast to working in football.

And Martin and I had a whale of a time, exchanging experiences in Californian wine tasting, sampling as many superb restaurants as we could find. It was such a tough life. To escape the worst of the heat, racing finished early in the afternoon. That left only four hours each day to work on a suntan!

I loved the rowing so I can't say I was disappointed but, oddly, we felt detached from the rest of the Olympics. The American media coverage, television and newspapers, was shamefully and shamelessly biased towards their own competitors. Trying to find out how the rest of the world was doing, never mind the Brits, was all too frustrating. You had to search very hard. I think the United States is the most parochial nation on earth, its inhabitants blissfully unaware of their own ignorance. It's my experience that many Americans know little of what goes on outside their own county, their own state. They're simply not interested. They assume they're the biggest and the best at everything and that's among their least likeable characteristics. It's a great place to go on holiday, as I do every year, but live there? There's no chance of that happening.

The atmosphere meant that we were constantly looking for opportunities, athletically at any rate, to embarrass our hosts. Every non-American took delight in the Yanks being beaten and particularly in the triple-gold success of Irish swimmer Michelle Smith. Janet Evans seemed nothing more than a whinger though, in retrospect, we must all hold our hands up and apologise. Smith, DeBruin as she is now, was subsequently found to have used banned substances.

Attitude matters as well. I sat with Martin in a sports bar having a meal on the night of the men's 100 metres final with a giant television screen relaying events from the Olympic Stadium. It was a very uncomfortable experience. Unlike the majority of the British public, I never took to Linford Christie, even when he was winning gold in Barcelona. The chips on each of his shoulders were always obvious to me. His behaviour, as the men's team captain, when he was disqualified that evening was a disgrace. We ate our food hoping that nobody would notice we were his fellow countrymen. Nobody in rowing would ever act like that, certainly not Redgrave and Pinsent.

They were obvious favourites to take the gold medal. Every boat racing against them was in awe of their presence. The Britons' supreme confidence bordered on arrogance but this was an arrogance that I could easily live with. I've never had a problem with anyone believing they are good when they also have the ability to match that belief. Everyone knew that Redgrave and Pinsent were the best. All they had to do was prove it by winning the Olympic final.

They cruised through their heats, dominating, overwhelming the opposition, and though the final of the coxless pairs was taking place on the Saturday morning, the penultimate day of the rowing competition, I knew that it would provide the true climax of the regatta. This was why I was in Georgia when, normally, I would have been somewhere else, probably on a beach.

I'm sure Steve and Matt didn't lose a wink of sleep the night before the race. Their heads hit the pillows comforted by the years of training that had prepared them for the moment. Unlike me. I was still a rookie rowing commentator but I, too, had to get it right. I tossed and turned in my bed but it was quickly obvious to me that there was no hope of getting to sleep. Around two o'clock in the morning, I gave up. I switched the television on, prepared to put up with the endless repeats of some American gymnastic or basketball success. Anything to kill time.

Instead, every television channel was tuned to the aftermath of the Atlanta bombing. I could hardly believe what I was seeing and I was too punch-drunk to assess the consequences for the Olympics. Could they continue in the circumstances? I was a little surprised to find that they would, despite the understandable reaction of not giving in to terrorism. Of course, this wasn't on the scale of the shooting that marred the Munich Olympics in 1972, but the whole of the United States was in shock that night – that such a thing could happen on their doorstep with the world looking on.

At 4 a.m. (five hours behind UK time) I rang home to tell my wife not to worry. I was nowhere near the scene of the outrage. I asked her to ring my parents to assure them of my safety.

At 5.40 a.m. my phone rang; it was Bob Shennan in Atlanta. He and the then head of 5 Live, Jenny Abramsky, had intended to travel out to Lake Lanier for the racing that morning, hoping to witness a British gold medal. Bob told me that there was a security cordon around their city centre hotel. Nobody was being allowed in or out. 'I'm sorry, Alan, we really wanted to come. We'll get out to you tomorrow. I just want to wish you all the best for the commentary. I have complete faith in your ability. Oh, one thing, Alan . . . make sure it's gold!' As if I wasn't feeling enough pressure.

I'm sure I felt more nervous prior to the race than Redgrave and Pinsent did. Even though I could never feel as comfortable commentating on rowing as I do on football, I'd resisted the temptation to script anything beforehand. This race was important to me, very important, but in terms of commentary technique it was no different. I also knew that in Martin, I had an expert sitting alongside me. I was also confident in my own ability, almost as confident as I was that the British boat would win.

The six minutes or so flew by and the race went like a dream. I felt the commentary went in tandem. As Redgrave and Pinsent crossed the finishing line, I declared: 'It's glory for Great Britain, their first gold of the Atlanta Olympics. It's glory, glory for Matthew Pinsent, another gold to follow the medal he won in Barcelona. And it's glory, glory and hallelujah for Steve Redgrave, a gold medal for him in four successive Olympic Games. Redgrave and Pinsent, R and P, rowing perfection!'

It may seem silly now but, once the microphones were put down, Martin and I embraced. We each had tears in our eyes. It was as if we, too, had spent countless hours, at ridiculous times, out on the river, stroke after stroke, in the gym in the depths of winter. Four years had been negotiated in preparation for this single moment of triumph. Of course, *we* hadn't, but the beauty of sports commentary is that people like me are in a position to feel that, somehow, we share in the success of others.

There was more pleasure to come. I ran down to the boat jetty, tape recorder in hand. Dan Topolski was already there, interviewing Steve and Matt, who were still in the boat, live on BBC television. I waited my turn. Mentally, I had calculated that the natural progression of the interview should be to talk to Redgrave first, move along to Pinsent, and then back to finish with Redgrave. I was conscious that an Australian TV interviewer was standing nearby. Like Topolski, he was live and preparing to move in to talk to Redgrave as soon as I shuffled along the deck to get to Pinsent. It wasn't his concern but it would ruin the flow of my interview if it happened. I had no choice. I moved towards Matt, hearing the Aussie introduce himself to Steve a couple of yards behind. 'Of course, I'll do the interview,' replied Steve, 'but I'm sorry, you'll have to wait until Alan's finished.' Redgrave, the ultimate professional in everything he does.

When I returned to Steve to wrap up the interview ('If anyone sees me in a boat again, they have my permission to shoot me!'), both oarsmen understood how genuine my thanks were. I turned to run to the broadcast point to send the recording back to London. As I did so, Matt shouted to me: 'Greenie, bet you're glad you came!' How right he was. Then Steve: 'Alan, sorry we couldn't give you a race.' I knew what he meant. Their victory over the Aussies hadn't been a race. It was a procession. Once more, I could feel the tears welling up.

Martin and I held our own private party that night, just the two of us, but what a party!

Redgrave didn't retire and the pair is now a four, James Cracknell and Tim Foster joining R and P's boat. Since then, I've described them winning three world championships at Aiguebelette, Cologne and St Catherine's. By the time you read this, I will have seen them in Sydney and I'm confident that, with the considerable help of his colleagues, Redgrave will create further Olympic history. Winning gold medals in five successive Olympic games is an astonishing and unprecedented achievement. He is, in my view, the greatest athlete that Britain has produced in any sport. It's our fault, yours as well as mine, that he's never been recognised as such. It's to Steve's eternal credit that he's not remotely bothered by the slight.

CHAPTER FIFTEEN

THE REFEREE'S NIGHTMARE

Dermot Gallagher, the much-respected referee from Banbury, had responded very positively to an invitation to appear on the Friday night programme that I regularly present on 5 Live. The necessary approval from the advisor to the Premiership referees seemed a formality. However, Phillip Don refused, without explanation. I really should have expected as much.

A couple of years ago, before the need for such an advisor, Keith Cooper did manage an appearance on the show. He was a referee I greatly admired because of the way he applied common sense in his application of the laws. Keith arrived at Broadcasting House well in advance of the start time so we had ample opportunity to discuss what was likely to come up once we went on air. I was delighted that he seemed so chatty, full of good humour and good stories. My only reservation was that he enlightened me as to my standing among Premiership officials. Whereas Sky Sports' Martin Tyler was perceived as 'the referee's friend', Keith said I was viewed as their 'nightmare'. I took it as a compliment. Far better, I thought, to be seen as a respected critic than some kind of sycophant. At least, that was my interpretation of what he said.

The shame was that Keith Cooper spent the following hour and a half almost entirely on the defensive. Much though I like the Welshman personally, his lack of candour during the programme definitely dictated my thoughts on any future appearances by referees. Most are as paranoid as managers – bluntly, I find their appearances to be worthless on air.

There are exceptions. Peter Jones from Loughborough is not only a very nice man, he's very good at his job. Having been privileged to get to know him, I understand well why he's so respected. What a pity there aren't more like him. Instead, the profession is populated by far too many poseurs and prima donnas.

I'm really too kind. I will spare the blushes of one particular referee by not naming him. He hadn't been on the Premiership list long. I was sitting in the press room at Southampton fully three hours before kick-off. John Motson was the only other person around and I'm not even sure Motty knew I was there. On match day, he tends to go into some strange trance. I've lost count of the number of times he's walked straight past me. I'm sure he doesn't mean to be that rude. He's simply entirely focused on the task ahead, oblivious to everything and everyone around him.

Anyway, in walked the referee. Ignoring me (he wouldn't have known me from Adam) he went straight up to John, hand outstretched: 'Hello, I'm X. Is there anything you'd like to know about me? My background, anything?' I thought: 'What a pompous idiot!' To this day, I can't think of that referee without recalling the crawling demeanour he assumed that afternoon at the Dell. He is, sadly, too typical of the breed, too conscious of how they are viewed by the public and perceived in the media. One has even gone so far as to employ an agent!

Nevertheless, I am surprised, and flattered, that referees are plainly concerned at what I say. So perhaps it's time I offered them a little reassurance. I have no hit-list or set ideas. Hand on heart, I never pay the slightest attention to who is officiating at any game until I get to the ground and read the programme to find out. Even then, as far as I am concerned, I don't think: 'Oh, it's X. What a botch he made of the game at Villa last week!' Honestly. I do try to blot out of my mind any previous misdemeanours, as I do with any team I watch. In my commentary, every referee starts a game with a blemish-free record. I'm only concerned with what they do during the next ninety minutes.

Of course, I'm not denying that I tend to be more critical of referees than most commentators. I don't believe, as some do, that they should be untouchable. Referees are vital participants in the game. Why should their amateur status absolve them from admonishment if they get things wrong? I see them as I do teams and players. I praise referees when they do well and criticise them if they don't. In that regard, I am no different from any paying punter in the stands. I know refs have a difficult job to do, increasingly difficult, but no one forced them into it. If they can't stand the heat of the kitchen, they have an option . . .

There are many ideas as to how to improve their lot and their performance. Naturally, some are better than others. For example, I have mixed feelings about turning the top referees into professionals. Unquestionably, it would free up time now needed in their regular jobs which, instead, could be spent visiting clubs and talking to players. Some of that goes on already, but not enough of it. If more referees took part in training sessions, stopping play so that they could directly explain why they've made certain decisions, there might be less questioning of officials during actual matches. It's possible, too, that being full time would make them fitter to cope with the pace of the modern game. And paying them decent money, rather than glorified travel expenses, might attract former players into the profession. However, you'd still have to recognise that referees don't last forever and that wherever you select the cut-off point in terms of age, it would most certainly take effect long before normal retirement at sixty or sixty-five. How would it be possible to pay them enough to cope with the consequent loss of earning years? Ask yourself if you would be prepared to give up a normal income and security for the privilege of being slaughtered by people like me over a period of years.

The main problem I foresee with full-time professional referees is that there can be no guarantee they will be better referees. So I prefer to look elsewhere for solutions.

Years ago, I was strolling in the Turin sunshine with the former England coach, Don Howe, killing time very pleasantly prior to an Arsenal game against Torino. I was giving full vent to my feelings about certain recent refereeing displays. Don, a very deep thinker about the game, told me he'd long believed that the answer lay in having two referees not one. I immediately liked the idea and ever since, I've argued that we should experiment with it, as the Italians have done fairly successfully in their cup competition.

Each referee would have specific responsibility for one half of the pitch. This, in itself, would cut out many of the physical problems referees have in keeping up with the pace of the modern game. What, you may wonder, would happen in the 'grey area' around the halfway line? Surely, cooperation would not be beyond the people concerned? Aren't two heads always better than one?

There is an obvious way, too, of helping a referee with an additional pair of eyes without needing another person on the pitch. Indeed, more than one pair. That's through using technology. It's hard on referees, I know, with the multitude of television cameras that cover games nowadays, exposing any error that they make. But, instead of griping about it, moaning that it's unfair, that they can't be expected to see everything and make the right decision every time, why not exploit that technology?

You don't have to go all the way. Using cameras to decide everything would leave the poor referee as nothing more than a pitch robot implementing decisions made on television gantries. That would be wrong in principle, making football a very different game by eliminating the human error which characterises the sport. It would be far less fun with far less cause for disagreement. What would be left to moan about? It would also entail far too many interruptions in play, checking whether an incident was a handball or a foul. No, we like our games to keep moving.

However, checking on matters of fact is something else. We should have electric eyes in the goalposts to indicate whether or not the ball has crossed the line. What significant time would elapse, too, for the referee to find out if a foul had been committed inside or outside the penalty area? Play is already held up anyway. Further, if a goal has been awarded and the player is offside, why shouldn't a fourth official up above communicate that information quickly so that the goal can be disallowed? I accept that we're venturing into radically new territory here but I'm certain, with sensible thinking, we can help and not hinder referees. Surely, these are the areas that cause great annoyance afterwards for teams and fans if the referee has made a wrong decision? Why not spare his embarrassment? After all, in Super League something similar happens, where referees can check that a try has been scored without any infringement taking place during the passage of play leading up to it. Such a system would help prevent assistant referees from being too ready to raise the flag for offside, where so many marginal decisions are made.

Yet the part of the game involving referees which provokes most resentment, and one of the most difficult to solve, is that of discipline and rather than blame the referees, I'd point the finger first at the authorities, but also at the players and their managers.

How often do we start a season with fresh edicts from FIFA or the Football Association about precisely what a referee should do in particular circumstances? Far too often, I would suggest. The result is that the poor referees are little better than annoying automatons awarding a free-kick for that challenge, a yellow card for this, a red card for that. It drives us all up the wall. The authorities leave them too little room for common sense and I know that many refs hate it.

We all know where the usual strict application of the laws in the first half of the season leads us. Referees are too quick to caution a first offence when a verbal warning would be enough. Showing an early yellow card dictates the approach to the game and leaves the referee prone to sending the same player off later, badly affecting matches through unjustified dismissals, and spoiling the game. Supporters see their team lose a player and then resort to all-out defence. Who benefits from that? I'm not saying players shouldn't be sent off when they deserve to be, as for serious foul play or persistent dissent, but is it really necessary for purely technical offences? I think not.

And then (doesn't it always happen?) those rigidities of early season turn into the relaxed rulings of springtime. What was a certain yellow or red card tackle three months ago might now barely warrant a ticking-off. It simply isn't good enough. Consistency must be the priority, from an individual referee and within a body of referees. Only then would we know where we stand.

But let's not allow the other participants to escape their responsibilities. Most managers will tell their players, as if they need encouragement, to push the boundaries back as far as they can get away with and this works at all levels, not just in the professional arena. You ask any referee of a Sunday league game. He'll tell you the same. A player will push a referee right to the limit and exploit the area that remains.

You see, the ultimate responsibility for discipline lies with those that play the game. We, on the sidelines, can moan as much as we like. Players are different. No referee's decision has ever been changed because a player argued against it. On the field, players should do what they're told, full stop. The sort of verbal assault that Andy d'Urso suffered at the hands of Manchester United during the Middlesbrough match at Old Trafford in 1999–2000 was entirely unacceptable. That is not part and parcel of the game. It was appalling, indeed disgraceful, that the FA did nothing about it. Whether or not the referee mentioned it in his report should have been merely incidental.

To that end, and breaking a habit by giving the Football Association some credit, I'm delighted that we're experimenting with the ten-yard rule. Actually, its application is long overdue. Even a cursory look at rugby would have shown any fool that it was worth implementing in football. I only regret that it has not already been deployed at all levels. It should and no doubt will be.

Referees are too important in football to be ignored. For me, their attitude and application of the laws needs to be born out of common sense. That goes for administrators and players as well.

CHAPTER SIXTEEN

TV AND FOOTBALL

My fourteen-year-old son berates me for refusing to succumb to his demand for digital television: 'Why can't we have Sky Digital? All my friends have it. I could see all the Champions League matches *and* the UEFA Cup. It won't cost much. Why can't we have it?'

'Listen, Simon,' as I scramble for reasons why not, 'we already have too much television to watch. I can't keep up with the output of four terrestrial channels [I still cannot take Channel 5 seriously and can't ever remember watching anything of value on it] never mind satellite. And now you want digital as well? You haven't the time to watch all the sport there is. Anyway, Sky Digital doesn't show the Champions League games, that's OnDigital.'

I've lost count of the number of such arguments that we've had. To be honest, I'm not even certain of my facts, though I am certain that one day soon I'll have to give in.

Simon lives in the golden age of televised football. When I was fourteen I remember watching the 1966 World Cup final on television.

I recall pacing round the front garden with my father at the end of normal time, both of us anxious for England's extra-time prospects. 'We've blown it. The boys must be devastated. The Germans will fancy it now more than us.'

That year, I suppose, also felt like a television treat. All those World Cup games to watch and we'd had a great FA Cup final live as well – Everton 3 Sheffield Wednesday 2. You see, then, the only live football on television was the Cup final, apart from the odd England match and, maybe, the likes of Austria against Hungary on a Sunday afternoon. Heaven only knows how Simon would have kept himself occupied in those distant days.

Today, you can watch football live on the telly seven days a week. Sometimes, on a Sunday, a casual flick of the remote control might bring you eight or more different games and that won't include the early morning second rendition of *Match of the Day*. The networks will tell you they're merely responding to demand, that people really want this much football on their sets, and I'm sure there probably is a significant number of addicts out there. I think they should see their doctors. Personally, watching that amount of football would drive me up the wall. So I don't.

I have Sky Sports. Yet I hardly ever watch any of their televised matches. I'm fortunate, very fortunate. If the game is really important, then almost certainly I'll be at it myself, and there are more than enough important fixtures to satisfy my appetite. If the game isn't important, and there are more than enough of those on the box as well, I probably won't switch on. I do have a life to lead outside football.

This goes even for something like the UEFA Cup. The last few seasons I've been so swamped with the Champions League demands on Tuesday and Wednesday evenings I can barely bring myself to watch, never mind attend, what's on the following night. UEFA themselves are partly to blame for that. They've managed to down-grade what used to be an outstanding competition, one that had a far greater depth of talent than the European Cup itself. However, as it is now, the UEFA Cup is merely a financial fallback for the clubs that fail to qualify for or fail to make progress in the Champions League.

The truth is there is a surfeit of football on television – far, far too much of it. I remember sitting in the kitchen one night and Simon rushed in, clearly excited: 'Why aren't you watching the game? Why didn't you tell me about it? Did you not want me to see it?'

'What game?' I was genuinely puzzled. It was a Thursday night and it wasn't a European week.

'It's Celtic against Bayern Munich,' he said, 'really good.' Yes, Celtic were playing the German champions, but it was only a friendly, in midwinter. Typically, Channel 5 chose to show it live and tried to beef up its importance by having the Scotland manager Craig Brown as an observer in the studio. Excellent though Craig is, even he couldn't save such a non-event. Simon switched off after a few minutes.

The trouble is, even if they know it, it's not in television's interests to admit that there is too much coverage of the sport. It is, after all, wonderful wallpaper. It fills acres of airtime. Where would Sky Sports be without football? Probably as bad as Eurosport is, with its truck-racing across the Sahara or synchronised bubble-blowing or whatever. And, increasingly, Sky sets the agenda for the rest of us. Part of the reason for the breadth of the football coverage on 5 Live is that frequently we follow their lead. Sky shows Nationwide League football on Friday evenings and at Sunday lunchtimes. We also broadcast those games. Sky allocates kick-off times to suit its schedules and its different sports channels. That's why 5 Live can end up commentating on four different games each Sunday. We're not complaining, and presumably neither is the audience or else we wouldn't be doing so. But it does have repercussions. In the mid-eighties, Mike Ingham and I were still scratching around, feeding on the leftovers from Peter Jones. Believe me, it was a treat then to get to commentate on a significant game. Nowadays, sometimes we struggle to find enough commentators to go round. Last season, 5 Live employed twelve different commentators and no one complained of a lack of work. There's often too much of it.

I frequently wonder about the editorial judgement behind broadcasting some matches. There's often a healthy discussion about the merits or otherwise of a particular game. Yet it's impossible to argue against the figures. Some people question the importance of many games they hear during the programme I present on 5 Live on a Friday evening but our experience is that football will always attract more listeners than the programme that would replace it. That's generally true of television as well. When Manchester United played South Melbourne in the Club World Championship in Rio de Janeiro the likelihood was they wouldn't be going any further in the competition. That expectation became fact, but 7.2 million people still tuned in to watch!

The question is, will that always be the case? As more and more football is shown on television and broadcast on the radio, will there still be as much interest? I'm not at all certain of that. I think there's a serious danger that if we dilute the product by showing more of it, it will not be as attractive. It used to be that television and radio billed their programmes as 'Soccer Specials' but what is special these days? Can Hertha Berlin against Chelsea in the Champions League have the same resonance as Manchester United versus Barcelona? Of course not. Yet we're continually being asked to believe that more equals better. My scepticism about this particular competition, and how it's been developed, is laid out elsewhere. Here, I need only refer to what the former president of AC Milan, Silvio Berlusconi, predicted many years ago. Berlusconi saw expansion of the European Cup as both desirable and inevitable. Nevertheless, he felt it would provoke a situation in which people would prefer to sit at home and watch the games on television. Television would therefore become the main source of revenue, not the paying spectators at the grounds. In order to attract big enough gates, to lend an atmosphere to these games, fans would have to be let in for free. Now, is that what we really want?

There are further dangers ahead if it's true that future generations of football fans will most likely be couch potatoes. If they can't be bothered to go to matches, who will take their sons? Then, will those boys still want to play the game? I see the danger in my own lad, who is far more likely to want to sit in front of his PlayStation or Dreamcast than attend an 'ordinary' game. If it's not Liverpool or Manchester United, he doesn't usually want to know.

Increasingly, television controls our view of football and its influence extends in some unhealthy ways. It has become a very distant memory – and you can call me an old fuddy-duddy if you like – but I loved the thought of going to watch matches at three o'clock on a Saturday afternoon, the era when most every game kicked off at that time, on that day. When both FA Cup semi-finals finished around a quarter to five on a Saturday. When the Cup draw meant gathering around a transistor radio at lunchtime on a Monday. You see, I'm old fashioned and proud of it. Television has changed all that. I think for the worse.

Then, even when television dictates the day and the kick-off time, they frequently fail to meet their own deadlines. It's not difficult to imagine players standing around waiting to start a vital fixture, pumped up with adrenaline, warding off the cold, while they wait for the referee to get the signal from the television stage manager that the advertisements are finished and the studio pundits have had their say. Yes, you can now kick off. It's not difficult to imagine because it happens most every Wednesday night or Sunday afternoon. We've all experienced that frustration. Well, how dare they. Why can't they get a simple timing right? Why should we have to wait for them? Don't tell me they couldn't start at the scheduled time if they tried just a little bit harder.

I honestly believe television doesn't understand that the best sport stands on its own and isn't dictated to. I know that I feel so much better as a broadcaster when I sense that I'm merely eavesdropping on a great occasion. That I'm being granted a very special privilege, just being there. To the contrary, clearly, today's relationship between television and football is a case of the tail wagging the dog.

Heaven forbid that we go further down the road towards the way Americans televise their sports. I think baseball is wonderful, but it's so controlled by television that almost the worst thing you can do is visit the stadium itself. If you do, prepare to be frustrated at the continual and lengthy disruption to the game caused by the television station showing its ads, trailing its programmes or allowing its jargon-filled commentators time to indulge themselves. Ball-players play when television tells them to. I despise it. Such a situation actually encourages you to stay at home, to watch the sport on television (their aim, I suppose) knowing that there will be plenty of inter-ruptions to do whatever else you might want to do. Americans, it seems, need such space. In my experience, most of them have the concentration span of a gnat. We don't need that here.

Of course, I'm not naïve. I appreciate that television has bought a product, football, and needs to recoup, indeed profit from its investment, by attracting advertisers. That's the business of com-mercial television. A product bought so expensively must, I understand, be 'sold'. But where do you draw the line? Can you afford to criticise the product? I can. No one ever tells me to imply that something is good when it patently isn't. I am encouraged to be entirely honest about what I'm seeing. I am your eyes. You must be able to trust me to tell you the truth.

Does Sky ever tell you you're watching a bad game? In the history of Sky Sports, have they ever broadcast a bad game? Now, I know, to a large extent, you can judge for yourselves but, believe me, clever camera work and constructive commentary can make you think that what you're watching is better than it actually is. The BBC can be guilty of this as well. It's in the very nature of highlights programmes to show only the best bits. When you edit the dross out of ninety minutes of football, the remaining ten can be made to look very attractive. It does represent the best of that game but can't possibly give you an accurate representation of what really happened.

You must forgive me if you feel I'm giving television too much of a bashing. I appreciate that for many people, the elderly, the sick, those too geographically distant from the event or those who can't afford to be there, television is their only opportunity to follow football. In that sense, we're offered a fantastic service. The depth and breadth of the coverage is phenomenal and Sky Sports is largely responsible for that. You could easily, if you wish, overdose on football and every aspect of life surrounding it. I wouldn't dream of criticising Sky for that. You can always switch off.

On the contrary, I think the time is ripe for football's governing bodies to tap into the benefits of that coverage instead of being frightened by it. Such is the intensity and sophistication of video technology, there can no longer be any sensible reason to ignore it when it comes to patrolling the sport. Of course, there has always been the argument that there aren't any television cameras on Hackney Marshes, that the overwhelming majority of games come under the sole scrutiny of the referee and a few spectators. That's true, but should that stop us using the technology that is available at the highest levels? After all, it's the highest levels that set the standards, which the whole of football tries to follow.

It needn't be so intrusive. While the game is in progress, the referee can, if he chooses, remain the sole arbiter of what's going on. But these people, in the ultra-quick game that football has become, need all the help they can get. I've never believed that referees' errors are all part and parcel of the game we love. Why should they be? Don't you hate it when they get things wrong?

The scenario after the game is quite different. In matters of fact, for example whether the ball has crossed the line or not, there can be no going back. That would lead to complete chaos. Wouldn't we have to replay the 1966 World Cup final? No, definitely not. But discipline is something else. If referees can't be forced to review their decisions about red or yellow cards, the authorities should do it for them, even more so when the referee, whether it's his fault or otherwise, has missed something entirely. It's nonsense to say that because so-and-so got away with that challenge in the Conference, where there was no camera, Smith or Jones or whoever should escape punishment in the Premiership where the camera saw it and the referee didn't. Players at top level must accept that their behaviour is under intense scrutiny. It's the way it is. If they feel it's unfair, I say that's just tough. They're paid enough money. Why shouldn't they behave themselves?

The television coverage is changing and expanding all the time. And football is wise to the financial opportunities. Look at how the Premiership was clever enough to break up the latest television contract negotiations into various packages (highlights, live action and pay-per-view) – all in the interests of raking in more money. And how they succeeded. Premiership television rights were sold for £1.64 billion over three seasons from 2001–02 to 2003–04. Don't be mistaken into thinking that it's only the television moguls that are worthy of our suspicion. The clubs are no angels themselves. Don't think either that the various media organisations buying their way into boardrooms up and down the country are doing so for altruistic motives. They smell money. They want to control who has access to the television rights at their particular club. They may want to restrict access or deny it altogether. Think: the only way a setup like Manchester United TV will truly succeed is if they get to do commentary on United's games, which is bound to eat into the access of Sky or ITV. Only the biggest clubs can succeed with such ventures.

The most exciting change, and the most imminent, will be the influence of the Internet. Standby to download coverage of the match you want to see directly to your computer screen or television or even your mobile phone. The technology is here. You'll have to pay, of course, but you're already used to doing that with Sky. The clubs won't know where to store all their money!

What you're seeing will alter as well. Sky Digital allows you to view matches from different camera angles. Or you can follow a particular player, though I'm at a loss to understand why anyone thought that was a good idea. And if you don't like that commentator, soon you'll be able to choose another. Exciting, isn't it? If only I was twenty years younger . . .

CHAPTER SEVENTEEN

ME AND TV

Whether it's by interviewers or punters, there are questions I'm asked so frequently that I now find it quite annoying. Perhaps it is meant to be flattering, but increasingly I ask myself if the questioner is trying to probe what they may perceive to be a problem area for me: 'Why are you not on television? Why aren't you doing TV commentary?'

I, and many others who work in radio, rather resent the implication that, naturally, we would wish to work in television and that there must be something amiss if we don't or don't aspire to. Rubbish. While it's true that a majority of broadcasters seem to see a move from radio to television as a progression in their career, it isn't so for all of us. Remember that I was a television commentator before I even thought about radio and I promise you, at no stage in making that transition, or ever since, have I felt that my career prospects were slipping.

Without digressing too much, let me tell you that the art of football commentary, if it is an art, is quite different in radio from the way it is in television. And someone who is good in one may not be as effective in the other. On radio, we must paint the whole picture, describing everything that the listeners would see for themselves if they were present. Not merely telling them what the score is, where the ball is and who's got it (though my advice to any aspiring radio commentator is to stick to those basics and let the 'embroidery' develop with experience), but also what the conditions are like, what's happening off the ball, and about that idiot in the row in front who's stood up trying to make an early exit to beat the traffic. You have to keep talking for most of the time while introducing breaths and pauses for dramatic effect.

Television requires a wholly different technique. Mostly, the action speaks for itself. The best television commentators, like Barry Davies, merely embellish the pictures with incisive background information or insight. They shouldn't talk for talk's sake. Unfortunately, there is a trend to do just that. If they're not burdening you with the breadth of their statistical knowledge ('That's the fifth goal Henry has scored this season with his left foot, three of them from outside the penalty area, and two of those were scored on Wednesday nights!'), most of which bores the pants off the viewers, then they're trying to impress us with their vocabulary. What does it mean, for example, to 'essay a cross'? Whereas some of them used to go to bed at night with a *Rothmans Football Yearbook*, I suspect now it must be a thesaurus they take with them!

And while I'm at it, let me nail another fallacy. Radio is not more difficult than television. Neither is the reverse true. They're simply different. And describing a boring 0–0 draw is just as problematical on radio as it is on television. A thrilling 3–3 is just as easy.

But I do digress, and, of course, I've been posed that question countless times. There's no point in false modesty. I know that I'm a good commentator. I don't believe there is any good reason why I couldn't make the move to television. Nor do I believe there's any good reason why I shouldn't have made that move, particularly since

I've seen some rather ordinary broadcasters move across. They know who they are and you should too.

So I think the question shouldn't be asked of me, rather of television. There have been approaches but not many. When Channel 5 was starting up their head of sport rang me and arranged a meeting. I was certainly interested. I was going through a spasmodic trough in my BBC career, as you do, wondering if I should be branching out or changing direction completely. And I was flattered at their interest. A new channel, perhaps with new thinking, fresh challenges; I didn't know but I was excited at the prospect of finding out.

I took the train down to London and a taxi to Channel 5's West London headquarters. The modern furniture of the offices contrasted markedly with the somewhat stuffy surroundings of Broadcasting House, though how we in Radio Sport miss BH now! I was ushered in to meet the Controller and the Chief Producer in Sport. I was what they were looking for, they said, the sort of 'in-your-face' broadcaster who would set a different agenda for television football commentary. They wanted me because I 'would appeal to the youth market' that they were aiming at. I was beginning to feel uneasy already. Certainly, I'm provocative, but 'in your face'? And I'd like to believe I have a broad appeal or, at least, that I'm liked or hated by all sections of the football community.

Still, there seemed no sense in dismissing them out of hand. What did they have to offer? Well, they said, how would I feel about doing Channel 5's first ever, and very expensively purchased, football commentary, Poland against England from Katowice? Yes, that would be nice, but I'm pretty certain of going to Poland anyway, what else did they have? Oh, there were negotiations under way to cover a pre-season friendly tournament at Elland Road and lots of other goodies were in the pipeline. Sorry, did you say 'friendly' tournament? Did they expect me to give up a well-established BBC career to cover one international and a couple of friendly matches? Sorry, you'll have to do a lot better than that. Would the BBC be willing, they asked, to release me from my contract to do the Poland game? Radio was at that point still negotiating for the rights to do the match themselves and Channel 5 implied that they'd be willing to help if radio agreed to allow me to work for them. Sorry, you'll have to ask them yourselves.

The meeting was going nowhere. I realised that BBC Radio would laugh in their faces. There wasn't the slightest chance of them releasing me to work for a competitor, particularly given the publicity that the move was likely to engender. If I was to consider resigning from the Corporation, and that was the only way I could do the Poland match for Channel 5, they'd have to come up with something else.

Out of the blue, how would I fancy presenting my own programme on the new network? Which programme? Well, we're not quite sure, that's for the chief producer to work out. Can he give you a ring in a few days' time? They would approach the BBC about a release for the international but they also wanted to put together a package that would encourage me to switch to them permanently.

I thought it an extremely ham-fisted, half-baked, naïve plan but there was little point in saying no at that stage. Channel 5 clearly wanted me.

A few days later an article appeared in the *Daily Mail*: 'Channel 5 Go For Green!' The guts of the meeting were in the piece but it seemed the BBC had already rejected the proposal to secure my release. I wasn't surprised. I would have done the same thing. The key was to be what else Channel 5 had in mind. For a start, we hadn't even discussed money.

I got the phone call. There was a possibility of me also co-hosting a weekend show but they could definitely offer me a late-night programme. What sort of programme? Aah . . . still not too sure about that. What would I be paid? How did I feel about £400 a show? I think he got the drift when I burst out laughing. Did they seriously believe I would give up the BBC for £20,000 a year plus Poland versus England plus a few friendlies? They'd have to think again. How would I feel about £600 a programme? What was going on here? Negotiations on the hoof? I suggested that he put the phone down and treat the matter seriously or don't bother at all.

He promised to ring back in a couple of days. I never heard from him again.

A few weeks later, Jonathan Pearce of Capital Radio was trumpeted as the new football voice of Channel 5, the new 'in-your-face' front for the network. He's a good lad, Jonathan, and a good friend, even if his style of commentary is very different from mine. However, I've never regretted that Channel 5 didn't ring back and targeted him instead. Though they have spent big money to cherry-pick certain football games, I didn't like their approach to sport then and I don't like it now. I listened to what they had to say but there was no serious prospect of me leaving the BBC for them.

Now, ITV I considered a more viable option, on more than one occasion. During the mid-eighties, when I still thought more highly of a future as an editor than as a broadcaster, I applied for a position in sport at Central Television. I attended an interview in Nottingham. Gary Newbon was chief, Geoff Farmer was his assistant. Their roles in ITV's football hierarchy are now reversed.

I thought I'd done quite well. Newbon told me he'd be in touch very soon, but there was no phone call, no letter, nothing. I heard on the grapevine that someone else had been appointed and that I'd been considered over-qualified for the post. It would have been nice to be told in person. I might even have tried to argue otherwise but I wasn't given the chance and felt let down by ITV and Gary Newbon (or whoever it was that should have contacted me).

I forgot all about them. Maybe they hadn't forgotten me. A few years ago, Newbon rang me at home.

Central Television, he said, was putting together a proposal for a new Thursday night football discussion programme, and he and his now boss, Geoff Farmer, thought that I'd be perfect to co-present it. Gary knew that I'd already heard about this from the agent Jon Holmes. It had actually been Holmes's idea, put to Newbon and Farmer, and rapidly taken up by them.

He was quite firm about their intentions. There'd be a pilot programme in September, but that was only a formality. The show was already in the schedules for a February start and a run of sixteen weeks. Newbon was so confident that he persuaded me to go ahead and tell my Head of Sport, Bob Shennan. I was freelance by this time and my contract would have allowed me to do almost anything except commentate for another broadcaster. This wasn't commentary, it was presentation. Bob gave his approval, though in fact, none was needed unless the work cut across any BBC commitments and, on a Thursday night, it didn't.

I went on holiday to the United States during August, excited at what I thought lay ahead. The pilot was to be recorded shortly after I returned.

It seemed to go reasonably well. Perhaps I should have treated myself to a haircut beforehand or to a re-style but Holmes, who attended, and was down to receive a percentage of any earnings, said he was happy, and Newbon and Farmer were both full of praise, at least to my face. I waited for their call. It didn't come.

There wasn't an explanatory letter, nothing. Up at Newcastle United for a Champions League game, I was even introduced to a television critic by Newbon as 'the new presenter of an ITV football programme'. But I heard nothing from Newbon or ITV. The programme did go on air, as planned, in February, but with Tony Francis as the main presenter. By now, however disappointed I'd become, I'd given up on Newbon. He hadn't the courtesy to explain why I wasn't suitable. He'd done it before.

Strangely and unexpectedly, the following summer, while England played in a World Cup warm-up tournament in France, Newbon sheepishly approached me in our hotel. I had never broached the subject with him but now, sensing his discomfort, and enjoying every moment, I asked him what had happened to the proposal that I present a football programme for ITV. Oh, Alan, you don't appreciate how conservative ITV is. We showed that pilot programme to the bosses at Central and they thought it would be too much of a risk taking on someone who'd only done radio; Francis was safe. I laughed. Newbon dug the hole deeper: 'Alan, if you're going to make it in television, then it'll be with the BBC. That's your natural way forward.'

So, why not the BBC? Ironically, there appears to be far less chance of moving into television within my own organisation than there is with any other outlet and I cannot give you a reason why. Only those within BBC Television Sport's set-up can offer an explanation.

During the mid-eighties I went on attachment to Television Sport. Still thinking I'd be best suited to a role away from a microphone or a camera, I'd applied for a position as one of two assistant editors.

I was the only serious applicant from outside the department but must have made a decent impact at the interview. I was telephoned afterwards by a member of BBC Personnel who told me that the 'board' had been very impressed and would have liked to appoint me directly to the position but that there were 'political factors' involved. Giving the job to someone like me, from radio, would cause enormous resentment within television. Therefore, they thought it more diplomatic if I went to work in television for a temporary period on attachment after which, assuming everything went well, I'd get the permanent position. I agreed.

I didn't appreciate just how much my presence would be resented. People within *Sportsnight* (a programme that then ran on BBC 1 on Wednesday evenings) at first didn't even speak to me. They acted as if I didn't exist. It was pathetic. For example, when the time came to get the teas in, inevitably I'd be offered a cup that was only half full, and cold. I was thoroughly miserable but determined to get my own back by showing them I could do the job. And I did.

At the end of the six months, Jonathan Martin, then Head of BBC TV Sport, called me into his office and offered me a position of Producer, Sport. I asked what had happened to the role of assistant editor and he explained that the editor, John Rowlinson, no longer felt that he needed an assistant. Martin asked me to be patient. Come in, at the lesser position, and a little time would sort everything out.

I felt let down. I'd left my family behind in Macclesfield (my daughter, Sarah, was only two years old) and come to London at their request. I'd put up with their infantile behaviour, and thought I'd proved I was equal to the task. However, Martin wanted me to accept less than I felt entitled to. I decided I was going back to radio.

It was a defining moment in my BBC television 'career'. By turning down this lesser opportunity, I have no doubt that I put some noses out of joint. Although I have become good friends with some of the BBC producers I worked with at that time, and who had been impressed with my work and determination, others, who've moved on to hold senior positions within Television Sport, became obvious enemies. They're the ones to ask why I've made no progress whatsoever within BBC television.

I regret it only in the sense that I would like to have proved them wrong. I honestly think I would have become a far better editor than I am a commentator. And I do wonder what might have happened if I'd got that job in 1985. As you've read, there were two positions as assistant editor. Brian Barwick became assistant editor of *Grandstand*. Later, he became BBC Television's Head of Football, then Head of Sport. That's his current position with ITV, where he is also Controller of ITV 2.

Why has no one taken me on as a television commentator? Again, you must ask television for the reasons why, though, naturally, I've tried to figure it out for myself. I hope I haven't taken too much for granted in believing I could do the job. So, perhaps, it's how I would do the job.

Certainly, none of my colleagues in television is as forthright as I have become. Some, I'm sure, would like to be, and certainly are when they're away from the microphone. However, you have to appreciate – and I do – that they are often burdened with their employer's concerns about contracts. Take Sky Sports. I've pointed out already how infrequently their commentators say what a bad game they're describing. Sky has paid a fortune to get the Premiership and, though I have some reservations, they do a wonderful job promoting it. But there's the rub; I am not a salesman. If the football that I am watching isn't good, I certainly won't be selling it to you. I believe that's the game's responsibility and not mine.

Of course, BBC Radio is just as interested in protecting its contracts. However, not once has anyone ever told me to say a game is better than it is merely to satisfy a sponsor or for fear of offending an authority or a club. I'm not saying that Sky or ITV or BBC Television asks its commentators to do so but there is undoubtedly a concern there not to offend. A senior Sky Sports employee once told me that they were always anxious to 'accentuate the positive'. He didn't give me a good enough answer when I asked if they were also allowed to 'mention the negative'.

Quite how at odds I am with the position adopted by Sky was made clear to me after the 1999–2000 FA Cup semi-final between Bolton Wanderers and Aston Villa. It had been an absolutely appalling game. Only if you supported either club could you have retained any interest. Certainly, I unsheathed my sword. At the start of extra time, I wondered out loud why we couldn't go straight to penalties. I bemoaned the fact that I had missed my flight home to continue to watch this drivel.

Now, this is a style I have. It's me. If I'm enjoying something, I think you'll know all about it. Even Manchester United fans, who otherwise normally question my 'bias' against their team, still refer to the excitement in my voice as I described the climax to that remarkable 1999 European Cup final. Yet if I'm not having a good time, you'll know that as well.

The fact is, during that Sunday afternoon at Wembley, the other commentator, Mike Ingham, and the summariser, Mark Lawrenson, were singing from the same hymn-sheet as I was. We all hated the game and said so in our different ways.

The following day I flew to Spain with Manchester United for a Champions League game against Real Madrid so I was unaware of the minor storm being generated back home by the Sky pundit, Andy Gray. He had been at Leicester City against Derby County, an earlier kick-off that Sunday, and was listening to 5 Live's commentary on the semi-final while driving home (I thought this strange in itself since Gray clearly preferred our coverage to that of the lamentable TalkSport, which occasionally employs him). What he heard upset him.

On the Monday evening, Gray chose his Sky platform to criticise

5 Live. He said our approach had been wholly negative and he talked about people broadcasting on football who had never played the game and therefore didn't understand it. It was a scarcely veiled attack on me and when the *Mirror* ran a substantial story on the Tuesday, the basis of which was 'Gray versus Green', Andy certainly did nothing to disabuse them of the notion.

I found his stance both arrogant and ignorant. He seemed to have forgotten, for example, what Mark Lawrenson had also said; the same Lawrenson of Liverpool and Republic of Ireland fame who, many would consider, had a rather more distinguished playing career than Andy Gray.

More to the point though, if the Scot really believed what he argued, then indirectly he insulted almost every single person who buys a ticket to watch a football match. How many of them played the game at any decent level? Clearly, in Gray's opinion, their views will count for as little as mine. You can widen the argument. Has Barry Norman any right to talk about the movie business when he didn't direct *Gone with the Wind*? And how dare they allow male gynaecologists into the operating theatre! How many of them have had a baby?

As Gray frequently reminds us, he did indeed play the game at the highest levels. I used to admire him as a player. I still recall a wonderful goal he scored at Notts County as Everton moved towards the FA Cup final of 1984. And I actually admire him, too, as a pundit even if he seems never to see a bad game on Sky. However, Gray scored a colossal own goal in criticising me the way he did. The response to the issue among *Mirror* readers who were asked for their thoughts was overwhelmingly in my favour, and I hope he will learn from that. I have no problems with Andy or anyone else disagreeing with my opinion, but people should respect my right to hold one.

I think I frighten television. I think they view me as a loose cannon whose commentary, however truthful, however popular, might lead to controversy that they can ill afford in the delicate area of contract negotiation. Better to stick with those that are safe. I understand. I only wish that I had an opportunity to show those who control television that blandness isn't best and that authorities and football clubs can withstand criticism when they see that it is based in fairness and in fact. Should we really worry about those who can't take any criticism? About those who cannot balance out criticism with the praise offered at other times?

I'm very, very happy in radio. They trust me. On the few occasions that I go too far, they rap my knuckles, and rightly so. You won't hear me moan. Television is clearly happy to do without me. The feeling is mutual.

CHAPTER EIGHTEEN

FOOTBALL'S IN FASHION

One day, during France 98, I rang home hoping to talk to my wife. Unexpectedly, it was my daughter Sarah who answered the phone. Now, I'm probably typical of fathers who have teenage daughters: there are problems. Let's say that Sarah and I were going through a phase during which we didn't have a lot in common. To be blunt, apart from blood ties and bills, we had nothing in common.

'Mum's not in,' she said. 'Do you want to leave a message?'

'No, it's all right. Tell her I called and that I'll ring back later.' Then, just as I was about to put the phone down . . .

'Dad? Do you think Glenn Hoddle should have had Michael Owen in the team earlier?'

I was stunned. Sarah had never, ever before shown the remotest interest in football. More to the point, I doubt that she cared what I did for a living except for knowing that it brought money into the house, a fair amount of it spent on her. Further, as she constantly reminded me, my career embarrassed the life out of her at school because most of her friends knew of me: 'Why couldn't you have been a teacher or an electrician or a postman? Anything but a football commentator!'

Anyway, I replied: 'Yes, of course he should have brought Owen in earlier. I'd have had him starting in the side long before Hoddle did.'

'Dad, do you blame David Beckham?'

'Mmm . . . to a degree. What Beckham did [against Argentina] was bloody stupid. But I don't think England would have been good enough to win the World Cup anyway and I certainly don't hold anything against him now or into next season. He knows he was wrong. He's only a kid; he'll learn. Beckham's a great player.'

'Don't you think it was unfair on David Batty? I mean, if Paul Ince had scored with his penalty, there wouldn't have been as much pressure on Batty.'

'Yeah, you're right, but . . . what is all this, Sarah? You've never talked to me about football in your life. What's going on here?'

'Oh, I've been watching all the games. Well, I've seen all England's games. I really like watching them play. I like Michael Owen and David Beckham.'

I was stunned: 'All right, love. I'll talk to you again soon. Tell Mum I called.'

I had to get off the phone. Really, I had to get up off the floor! What was this? Sarah? Interested in *football*?! I suppose I should have seen it coming. For years I'd been talking about how 'in' football had become. Of how its participants had become interesting far beyond the sports pages. Of how you are as likely to see David Beckham photographed in a sarong or a bandanna as in his working clothes. Usually, more so. It's obvious: football is fashionable. Footballers, particularly certain footballers, are newsworthy in ways their equivalent wouldn't have dreamed possible forty years ago.

★   ★   ★

It was Manchester United's George Best who started this revolution in attitude: 'Bestie', 'Georgie the Belfast Boy', 'the fifth Beatle'. George moved the image of the sport off the back pages and into the consciousness of the nation's youth, even to the attention of those who wouldn't normally give a second's thought to football. You simply couldn't ignore him, on or off the pitch. You see, apart from being one of the greatest players the world has ever seen, Best epitomised the Swinging Sixties; its hairstyles, its dress sense, its excesses. And George knew better than any of his contemporaries how to have a good time. Further, he wasn't ashamed or embarrassed to let the world eavesdrop on his playtime. The papers were full of him, pictured in this bar or that nightclub, with this brunette or, more likely, that blonde. I wish I'd been of his generation as a reporter or commentator. There would have been a lot of fun around.

Now, for different reasons, I don't know David Beckham. From what I gather from people who do, he's an extremely nice lad who, if anything, is rather shy. But he hardly hides from his public and don't tell me that you can't. Alan Shearer was England captain but kept much of his private life away from public scrutiny. Michael Owen's private affairs remain mostly his own. Beckham is different.

No doubt orchestrated by his other half's vast publicity machine, Beckham never escapes the attention of the media. Actually, he sometimes courts it. Are we to believe that he isn't enjoying himself? That he'd rather retreat into anonymity? That, financially, he doesn't make a fortune from it? After all, what a nice quiet wedding! How much did *OK!* pay for those photographs? I'm sure the cheque must have helped with the electricity bill. People who put themselves in the public eye can't have their cake and eat it as well. My daughter couldn't tell me anything about Beckham's footballing ability, about that fantastic right foot or his free-kicks and phenomenal work-rate.

But she sure as hell knows what he was wearing the other night. I simply don't believe that he hates all the attention.

And the clubs don't complain about these distractions, though their managers might. The more publicity their players receive, the more fashionable they become, the greater the crowds pouring into those club shops, the more demand there is for the executive boxes. That is football today. A highly desirable item of fashion. A monster of publicity spawning a financial feeding frenzy. And there is much to dislike.

Take those executive boxes. I do wish someone would. I appreciate that they draw in substantial income, and provide a very popular venue for businessmen, allowing them profitably to mix work with pleasure. But they are an abomination in terms of what they've done to the atmosphere at many of our grounds.

Only once have I watched a game from such a highly privileged position. I'm almost ashamed to admit it, but I had a great time. However, I'm certain it was the exception that proves the rule. I was a guest for a match at Anfield. As I sat through the meal, enjoying the food and the wine and the company, I began to feel guilty. This, surely, wasn't what watching football should be about, isolated from the crowd and the noise and the smell of dodgy burgers and Bovril. Fortunately, the people I was with were as passionate about the resulting game as I was. So we screamed and we swore and we abused the referee as much as the next person. But I knew afterwards that it wasn't, and could never be, my scene. Unlike my steak, I like my football raw.

At least, some of the business people who go to games nowadays do care. I'm far less convinced about many of the politicians and those from the world of entertainment. Think how many of these 'fans' have crawled out of the woodwork since football became fashionable. Their example makes me shudder. I've always voted

Labour, and will continue to do so, but shouldn't a spin doctor have checked the facts before Prime Minister Tony Blair 'remembered' sitting at the Gallowgate end of St James' Park as a young boy? Maybe the PM did sit on the Gallowgate, but he'd surely have had trouble seeing the match through the legs of all those people standing in front of him. Terraces, Tony, not seats. These people seek popularity by associating themselves with the game. I'm not talking about obviously genuine fans like Roy Hattersley, whose blood runs Sheffield Wednesday blue, but I truly despise those ex-politician phone-in hosts and female disc-jockeys whose love of football does not go as deep.

If following football is increasingly fashionable, it's also increasingly middle class, particularly at the highest levels where you need to earn a small fortune to be able to afford to go to matches, and especially if you are trying to take your family with you. I'm not knocking the middle classes. How could I? I'm 'middle class', but my feelings for football are cutting edge 'working class'. People say to me: 'You get so worked up in commentary.' Well, they should see me when I'm not restrained by a microphone! But that is not a middle-class reaction. The middle classes are often, in their very nature, restrained. Hence the subdued atmosphere at too many grounds. I suspect that as it costs more to go to football, less noise will be generated by the crowd. More money, less passion. Go see a game at a lower level, where it's cheaper, and you'll see what I mean.

Sarah has been to games. With specific aims in mind. One wish, to meet Jamie Redknapp, came true. It was as if she had found herself face to face with Brad Pitt. Another, to ask Jamie's pop-star wife Louise where she has her hair done, is as yet unfulfilled. Sarah's priorities were far different from mine but many of them matched those of a similar age group that's currently drawn to the fashion of football. To them, the match itself may be immaterial, and I find that sad.

Yet I mustn't deride everything merely because it is fashionable. For example, I happen to love people wearing replica shirts to games. Is there a more inspiring sight in the whole of English football than to sit at St James' Park (sit, Tony) and see nine-tenths of the crowd dressed in black and white stripes? They're like a magnificent herd of zebra.

Of course, this particular fad has penalties. It's all right for the likes of me, who can well afford to clothe my son in the latest kit of his favourite football team, or in Simon's case, teams. But what of those who can't? It's easy for manufacturers to say no one is forced to buy their products. Perhaps they don't have to look into the imploring eyes of sons and daughters anxious for a new shirt simply because the team sponsor has changed and what they're wearing is now out of date, because that isn't easy.

On the other hand, kids wear these shirts so often that what is, initially, a considerable financial outlay, may in the long term be quite good value. What does bug me though is the irresponsibility of certain clubs who commission too many kits and change them too often. Football authorities are charged with looking after the interests of supporters as well as clubs. They should regulate in such areas. Then, there'd be far less resentment from the public.

Trouble is, and the manufacturers know it, replica kits are not selling as well as they once did. Perhaps the reach is already so great that the market is at saturation point and the number of kit changes reflects concern within the industry that sales are dropping. How many shirts does any one child need? Are parents buying them bigger in an effort to make them last longer and are children being persuaded that a change of sponsor and a minor alteration to the sleeve or the collar doesn't really matter? Do they still want to eat breakfast in the morning?

Of one thing I'm certain, and the sale of replica shirts is a good example, kids won't always have them at the top of their wish list. Something else will someday hold a greater attraction. Football and its many by-products won't always be fashionable. If the clubs and their commercial managers don't grasp this point they're heading for a colossal shock and a mighty fall. I keep on repeating this, because it's vital. In too many ways, football is forgetting its hard-core support. Forgetting those who couldn't care less of an evening where David Beckham goes or what he wears or how he has his hair cut. What they care about is what Beckham does when he climbs into his work clothes. Football ignores that, and them, at its peril.

CHAPTER NINETEEN

A POISONED CHALICE?

'I've known five different England managers since I first properly started to follow the fortunes of the national team a decade ago. Though I understand why each of them was drawn to the job – it would take a peculiar Englishman *not* to want to manage his country – nothing I've observed has changed my opinion that they must be half-crazy to subject themselves to the problems and pressures that the position entails.

Initially, until 1990, I knew only those who looked after the two Irelands. Those jobs attracted far less attention and, consequently, must have been a lot more fun.

You'll have read how I did some television commentary before I joined BBC Radio Sport. These were matches involving Irish League teams playing in Europe and the Irish Cup final. I also commentated on Northern Ireland games, which is how I first met Billy Bingham. Billy had played in the 1958 side that had reached the quarter-finals of the World Cup in Sweden, an astonishing achievement for such a small country. Yet, if anything, his achievements as international manager surpassed even that. Bingham took Northern Ireland to the final stages of two successive World Cups – Spain in 1982 and Mexico in 1986. Cynics would point out that he had some good players to work with: Pat Jennings, Martin O'Neill, Sammy McIlroy, and so on. But the eighties squads didn't have the talent of the one that Bingham himself had played in: Danny Blanchflower, Jimmy McIlroy, Peter McParland, Wilbur Cush and Harry Gregg. No, Bingham deserves huge credit for what he did as Northern Ireland boss.

Bingham was sharp as a pin, off as well as on the pitch. During the 1982 campaign, the media that followed Northern Ireland stayed in the same hotel as the team. We were one very happy family together. Of course, the reporters had rather more leeway to enjoy themselves than the players did. Two nights before Northern Ireland were due to play the hosts Spain in a critical match in Valencia, the reporters decided to go en masse to a nightclub. The Spanish Football Association had assigned a chaperone to the party and, to our delight, she led us past the bouncers and through the door . . . without paying. When questioned as to how she'd managed this, she laughed and said that she'd told the manager of the club that we were the Northern Ireland team. Hard though it may be to believe, some of us actually looked fit enough to pass as players. 'Get those beers in!'

The following morning, the day before the match, the daily press conference overflowed with Spanish reporters. Even Bingham looked slightly taken aback by their numbers. 'What do you think, Señor Bingham,' asked one, 'about your players spending half the night in a nightclub?' The manager didn't even blink: 'I have no problem with that. I encourage my players to relax, especially before huge games like this one. If they want to have a few beers, go dancing, I don't mind at all.' The Irish media didn't know where to look.

When the Spanish journalists had had their fill, Bingham politely asked them to leave so that he could deal with the requests of his regular reporters. As the last Spaniard left, Bingham looked around at us: 'What were you bastards up to!?' Rather sheepishly, we told him what had happened but all he did was laugh himself silly.

Billy was generally well liked but he did have a reputation for being somewhat on the mean side. Behind his back, he was known as Billy 'Bungham' – not as in brown envelopes – and we used to say that he worked for 'FIFA' – it was a fee for this and a fee for that! In truth, I never noticed too much of this, but I do remember vividly the night that Northern Ireland beat Israel at Windsor Park in Belfast to qualify for the 1982 World Cup finals. I was so proud. It had been a quarter of a century since my humble little part of the globe had done such a thing and here I was, commentating on it. Now, I had my arm around the manager as I led him down the touchline towards the camera where I would do the post-match interview. 'Alan,' he said, 'could you get me £200 for this?' I was too shocked to be polite. 'Billy, you can't talk about money at a time like this. I'll try to sort it out later.' I still admired Billy Bingham enormously.

Jack Charlton, though, became an even bigger subject of my affection. Between the Mexican World Cup and Italia 90, BBC Radio switched my affiliation from North to South and I attended to the affairs of the Republic of Ireland. 'Big Jack' was in charge, and how. The Irish, the nation as much as its players, quickly forgot that he was a hated Englishman. Worse, he was an English World Cup winner. Charlton's charm and wit and personality totally overwhelmed them. This was a marriage made in heaven. The Irish loved him and still do. They laughed at his willingness to call a spade 'an effing shovel' and respected his ability for drawing the maximum out of each and every player.

Jack had a reputation for meanness too. He'll happily admit that he was never the first to put his hand in his pocket when the call came for a round of drinks. Who cared? His company was worth every penny. And he never had a pack of cigarettes on his person. I didn't mind that either, as I didn't smoke.

The Irish fans, one of the best-behaved groups of supporters you'd ever wish to find yourself trapped among, simply adored Jack. I recall how, after the Republic had won an important match in Malta, Jack toured the pubs in Valletta to offer them his personal thanks. Jack was out all night and never had to buy a drink. Everyone was happy.

There was one rumour, though, whose truth or otherwise I never quite established. It held that Jack would go into any pub in Ireland and try to buy a drink. As if they'd let him. Then, as the party continued around him, Charlton would ask the landlord if he wouldn't mind cashing a cheque. Of course he didn't. Nor did the landlord ever present that cheque to the bank for payment. Instead, he pinned it above the bar, proudly pointing to the signature with every new customer: 'Big Jack's had a drink here!' I wonder if Charlton ever knew.

He's a wonderful man. I've never had the slightest cause to dislike him and he's been very good to me. Two incidents stand out. Before the 1990 World Cup, I arranged to see Jack in Dublin so that I could do a big interview with him. Ireland were playing Finland in a testimonial match for Liam Brady and Jack agreed to meet me at the team's hotel near the airport at lunchtime on the day of the game. My plane from Manchester was late.

I feared the worst as I approached the hotel's reception desk. Friendly or not, you don't mess around a manager or his players so close to a game. I asked the clerk to ring Jack's room. It was three and a half hours to kick-off. He handed me the telephone. 'Hello, who's that?'

'Jack, it's me, Alan. I'm sorry I'm so late. The plane was delayed.

I'll understand if you say no but can we still do this interview?'

'What interview?' It was going from bad to worse; Jack was in his bed. He'd forgotten all about the interview. Now, this didn't really surprise me. He had the most appalling memory (forgetting his name, he often referred to Tony Cascarino as 'the ice cream salesman'). Nevertheless, Jack, being Jack, said he'd still see me. When? 'When I get up out of bed about three o'clock.' He said he'd come to my room.

I was still worried and I was worried more at a quarter past three, for there was no sign of Jack. The hotel hadn't given me his room number and there was no answer when they put me through to his phone. I started to wander the hotel corridors hoping to stumble into him. I did – he'd forgotten which room I was in.

We sat down. 'Jack,' I said, 'I'm really sorry about this. It's all my fault. I don't think we've got enough time to do this. It's too close to the game.'

'How long do you need?'

'At least fifteen minutes.'

'Ah, that's all right. The bus can wait. It won't go without me – I'm the manager.'

I felt so guilty. It was four o'clock when we finished. Just an hour to kick-off. How was the coach supposed to get to Lansdowne Road in time? It was the other side of Dublin, and would have to go through the rush hour!

'Are you coming to the game?' he said. I told him that I had intended going but it was too late now to collect my ticket from the FAI headquarters. 'Stuff that!' said Jack. 'Come on the bus with the boys.'

I can't tell you how embarrassed I was climbing on to the coach behind Jack. All the players were laughing and gently teasing him. They'd been sitting around for half an hour. 'Shut up you lot! Right, off we go.' The police motorcyclists performed a miracle and somehow we got to the ground in time for the game. Jack walked me in with the players, so typical of the man.

During Italia 90, Ireland stayed for a while on Sardinia at a hotel only a couple of kilometres from England's base. There was a vivid contrast in the security deployed around the two camps. England maintained something of a fortress mentality. Only by pre-arrangement, or in exceptional circumstances, did you pass the 'guards'. Ireland's hotel was open house. It was just as well for me as I'd interviewed Charlton and returned to my own hotel only to find that, for whatever reason, it had been recorded at an absurdly low level. We needed the interview badly. It was the day before Ireland were to play England in the opening match of the group. I had no choice but to return to the Irish hotel and beg forgiveness; hopefully Jack would oblige once more.

The whole squad was out sunbathing on a small private beach. Jack stood alone on a rocky ledge staring out across the Mediterranean. I'm afraid he looked like the typical Brit abroad: bare-chested, white shorts, brown shoes and socks, and a green peaked cap. He was smoking a huge cigar and probably wishing he was out on some boat fishing. He caught sight of me out of the corner of his eye. 'And what do you want?' I explained my predicament. Most managers would have said 'That's tough' and brushed me aside. Jack asked only where I'd prefer to do this second interview.

I think he liked to give the impression that he wasn't quite on top of everything that he should be. Once, in Rapallo, before Ireland were due to meet Romania, he was asked at a press conference who in the opposition team was he impressed with.

'Oh, I don't know . . . I don't know their names.'

One journalist piped up: 'If you don't know their names, Jack, their numbers will do.'

He thought for a second or two: 'Ah, that little fella in midfield . . . the number ten. He can play.'

Jack knew very well how good a player Hagi was. He had him marked tightly in the game that Ireland famously won on penalties to see them through to a quarter-final clash with Italy.

Those who saw Charlton, with that faltering memory and superficial grasp of detail, as something of a fool misunderstood the man. He was fooling them. The great Johan Cruyff thought Charlton was one of the very best international managers.

In 1990, though I stayed with the Irish until they were knocked out, I also commentated on England's games. I'd only really come across Bobby Robson once before. That was in Tbilisi in 1986 when England played the Soviet Union prior to the Mexican World Cup. I was accustomed to the relaxed informality of the two Irelands. This was very different.

I attended my first ever England manager's press conference the day before the game. It was held in a dark, gloomy room at the most depressing hotel I'd ever stayed in. It's as well I'd been given some warning. Otherwise, I'd have been astounded that Robson was as gloomy as the venue.

It seemed to go on forever though, perhaps, that was down to the atmosphere. Within minutes, I realised what this job had already done to one of the nicest men in football. It wasn't merely that Robson's hair was prematurely greying, it was his general demeanour. Head down, suspicious of the most innocent questions, and given to extraordinary rambling answers.

He had already announced his team but, and I still don't know why, no one asked him about his then somewhat controversial selection of the mercurial Chris Waddle. I decided that I would, but lobbed the subject into the discussion as gently as I could:

'Waddle's in the team . . .' letting it hang there.

'Yes,' replied Robson, 'he is.' He looked away, inviting no further discussion on the topic. I got the message.

So, four years on, I was primed to be wary of Robson's responses. The day after Ireland held England to a punishing 1–1 draw, Robson came to the media base at the Forte Village as he'd indicated that he would. I think he'd been expecting to come on the back of a win and now regretted being so amenable. It was a rather edgy press conference. Halfway through it, I put my hand up. Robson looked in my direction. 'Given yesterday's scoreline, is there a result in tonight's match [Holland against Egypt in the same group] that would suit England best?'

'I don't have to answer that question,' snapped the retort, 'and I won't.' I was dumbfounded. There was no edge to the question, nor any hidden agenda. This, I decided, was a man under considerable pressure.

The conference broke up in farce. The representative from the *Daily Sport* ('London Bus Found On The Moon') asked Bobby what he thought of the advertisement hoardings. 'What?' said Robson.

'The hoardings. What do you think of the advertisement hoardings?'

'What are you on about?'

'Are they too close to the pitch?' This, of course, was the burning issue of the day. Robson, like all of us apart from the questioner, shook his head, made his excuses and left. On the day after the final, I bumped into the *Sport* reporter at Rome airport and gave him a prized BBC World Cup badge as a reward for asking the craziest question of the tournament. To his credit, he saw the funny side and immediately pinned the badge to his lapel.

The previous night, I spotted the England manager standing alone a few yards from our commentary position inside the Olympic

Stadium. He'd been working for television and was now gazing wistfully across the venue. I couldn't tell for sure, but I guessed he was thinking that it might have been England out there. That, after all, was what we'd all been thinking. I got up from my seat and walked across. 'Mr Robson, I'm Alan Green from BBC Radio Sport. I hope you don't mind me coming up, I just want to say thank you. I don't know if you appreciate just how proud you've made us all feel.' I turned and walked back to my seat. This time, he was the one who looked dumbfounded.

I really regret that I came on to the England scene near the end of Bobby Robson's spell in charge. Though he undoubtedly had his quirks, I'm sure I would have enjoyed being in his company. His honesty and love of the game always shines through. Given time, he might even have discovered that I was a 'foreigner' he could trust.

Graham Taylor seemed an ideal choice to succeed Robson. Probably, he was the only choice. Of the two other candidates actively considered, Joe Royle hadn't quite cut it at the top level and Howard Kendall, as he himself realised, had other problems. Taylor offered no such concerns. He was universally regarded as approachable, friendly and thoroughly decent. He was also a successful club manager, taking Watford from nowhere to Wembley and into Europe, and doing almost as well at Aston Villa. The only question was whether or not he could be equally adept on the international stage.

At the beginning, all went well. England were unbeaten during Taylor's first dozen games in charge, a run broken only by the old enemy, Germany. They also qualified for the 1992 European Championship in Sweden. But none of this was achieved with any style or, at least, style that the media appreciated. The long-ball approach, so successful at Vicarage Road, was frowned on when adopted by England. Graham seemed to have a penchant for players that others saw as merely hard-working, people like Carlton Palmer and Geoff Thomas. Very few in the press saw either as worthy of being capped by England and began questioning the judgement of anyone who did.

There was a suspicion among the media, too, perhaps unfounded, that Taylor was uncomfortable surrounded by talent, like Chris Waddle and Gary Lineker. Waddle was surely discarded too soon, while Lineker was amazingly substituted in the European Championship match against Sweden with England a goal down and Lineker a goal away from equalling Bobby Charlton's international scoring record.

By that stage, most of the media had turned on Taylor. It was a remarkable transformation. Taylor's father had been a journalist, so Graham had grown up in journalistic surroundings. He knew what reporters required to do their jobs and was certainly lucid and intelligent enough to meet their every desire. If anything, he was too amenable. But, as selections became more questionable, and tactics more unfathomable, we began to doubt Taylor's ability to do his job.

'Swedes 2, Turnips 1' was an immeasurably cruel headline in the *Sun* (the manager had earlier been cartooned as a 'turnip head'), but funny nevertheless. It may be easy to say but I so wished Graham had laughed it all off. That he had stuck that cartoon drawing on the wall behind his desk at Lancaster Gate. But he didn't. He had already stopped enjoying the work or, if not the work itself, certainly the circus that surrounded it.

The following two years, that included non-qualification for the 1994 World Cup in the USA, were painful. Taylor struggled trying to prove us all wrong. Along the way, he got so much wrong. I will never forget the fiasco in Oslo. England had, rather fortuitously, drawn in Poland a few days earlier. Now, a win away to Norway would set them back on course to qualify. Unfortunately, it was also a signal to trigger the more eccentric side of Taylor's approach.

The build-up was eerily tense, illustrated well by what happened at the time of England's final training session. This was to be held at the Ullevaal Stadium itself. It's quite normal for teams to go to the match stadium on the day before the game. It is, usually too, a 'closed' session. No journalists, even friendly ones, are allowed to witness those last-minute free-kick routines or tactics that might prove crucial. Heavens, they might leak the evidence to the enemy. Or so, daft though I think the notion is, most managers seem to believe.

I stood by the coach as the England squad trooped on board. The door closed and then, as I was about to walk back inside the hotel, it opened again. Out jumped the elderly representative of the Norwegian FA who accompanied England on the trip as a genuinely helpful guide. He rushed into reception, shaking his head. Taylor had just informed him that England had decided they wouldn't go to the stadium after all. They'd decided to train elsewhere and the guide now had to telephone the Ullevaal to let the groundsman know as much. Suddenly, I heard the coach door close again, the engine revving, and off they went. The Norwegian guide hadn't a clue what was going on except that he'd been deliberately left behind. It had all been a ruse to get rid of him. England trained, as secretly arranged, at a nearby NATO base away from any possible prying eyes.

Much good it did them. Taylor, so paranoid about the threat of the tall Jostein Flo on Norway's right wing, played Manchester United's Gary Pallister as a left-back. I will never forget the bemused look on Pallister's face when Flo started the match on the other side of the field. He looked to the England bench as if to say: 'What am I supposed to do now?' As if Taylor knew; his tactics were all over the place. It was one of the worst England displays that I've ever seen. Norway won 2–0.

Graham left himself so open to criticism, even when he was no longer in the job. His agreement to allow a fly-on-the-wall television documentary to accompany England's failed qualifying campaign wasn't the brightest of decisions. His scampering up and down the touchline in Rotterdam as Holland beat England left all of us with the most ludicrous images of his time in charge. I won't forget, either, the embarrassed laughter in the press area when San Marino took the lead against England in the final match in Bologna. It was either laugh or cry.

I felt so sorry for Graham at the end. It wasn't that he had such a bad record – won 18, drawn 12, lost 8 – more that he seemed to lose every match that mattered. Nor is he a bad manager, though he was clearly hapless in the international arena. Graham's a fine man whose manner deserved a better fate. I hated the fact that he was so clearly and deeply hurt by his experiences as England boss. I hope he understands that, for many of us, the criticism extended in his direction was professional and not personal.

I never got remotely as near to his successor, Terry Venables, despite as much opportunity. My contact always felt superficial. It wasn't that there was no depth to the man, far from it. There were some areas where you felt Venables was so deep as to be dangerous. Right from the off, for example, many at the Football Association shuddered at his various business dealings. Yet there's no question Venables was absolutely brilliant with the media. That's one of the reasons why a considerable section of the trade still hankers after his return. But I don't think he actually trusted or liked that many of us.

Generally, I liked the teams he produced though his popularity among journalists weighed so heavily that there was a definite tendency to overrate his achievements. What happened in Euro 96 is a prime illustration. It was forgotten then, and still is, that England won only two games out of five. The glorious victory over Holland seemed to dull the senses against more painful memories: that struggle against Switzerland in a far from convincing opening game; that Spain were clearly the better team in the quarter-final. Ultimately, that England lost on penalties to a very ordinary German side. I was one of the very few who pointed all of this out and wasn't caught up in the national hysteria, 'Three Lions on the Shirt' and all that nonsense. I remember listening to David Mellor's 5 Live phone-in on the way out of Wembley after the semi-final. One caller suggested I should be made to apologise to the nation for being so downbeat about England's performances. That man knew as much about football as the programme's presenter.

Yet there was undoubtedly something vibrant about the way England played under Terry Venables and he was the only England manager to draw the best out of Steve McManaman, whose talents are still squandered at international level. It would have been fascinating to see how England would have progressed under Venables. Instead, his off-the-field activities got in the way and in came Glenn Hoddle.

I'd be lying if I said that I wasn't initially impressed. For a start, the man's playing credentials were impeccable, easily one of the outstanding footballers of his generation. He looked a highly promising coach too, doing well at Swindon and even better at Chelsea, setting in motion the sweeping changes at Stamford Bridge that first Ruud Gullit and then Gianluca Vialli built on with such success. I thought he'd prove a fine choice as England boss.

But, even as we applauded England's progress under Hoddle through the World Cup qualifying campaign for France 98, little things happened that made me feel slightly uneasy. I didn't talk to him that often. Interviews were usually down to Mike Ingham or the producer. However, when I did chat to him, I found Hoddle invariably pleasant and thoughtful. Then again, listening carefully to what he said, I found myself wondering if his natural confidence wasn't plain arrogance. It was obvious that Hoddle felt he knew far better than anyone else did, whatever the subject.

There were also those annoying occasions when he would say something and then deny that he'd said it. Long before his infinitely more important ramblings about reincarnation and the disabled, I recall his words about Michael Owen prior to an England friendly match against Switzerland in Berne. Hoddle clearly stated that the Liverpool striker 'wasn't a natural finisher'. All the journalists who were present looked around, in a way asking each other if they hadn't misheard the England coach. It seemed such a ridiculous thing to say. Could he really have said it? Yes, he did. Some of us had it recorded. Yet that didn't stop Hoddle claiming that he hadn't, or that his words had been misunderstood, or that they'd been taken out of context. Hoddle was so much cleverer than those he spoke to, or so he seemed to think. In certain areas, this began to be very annoying.

I had no problem whatsoever with his fixation over Eileen Drewery, provided it remained personal. But it didn't. Hoddle brought the subject into the public domain and seemed genuinely bemused that so many people found his behaviour odd. Again, it was in keeping with his arrogance. And he never knew when it was best to say nothing. One of the worst features of that appalling, misconceived World Cup diary was his pronouncement that the biggest mistake he'd made was not taking her with him to France. What were we to believe? Would Eileen have willed Paul Ince or David Batty to have scored from those penalty kicks? The way she clearly determined that Ian Wright's shot hit the post in the crucial qualifier in Rome? Really, it was beyond belief.

At other times, he'd do something that I totally agreed with. Bobby Robson declared Paul Gascoigne 'daft as a brush'. Graham Taylor queried his 'refuelling habits'. Terry Venables patently indulged the man-child. Hoddle dumped Gascoigne quite ruthlessly. I thought it was a brave decision and a correct one.

Going into the tournament, I was prepared to put my reservations about Hoddle to one side. Anyone who had the wit to drop Gascoigne had my support. It didn't last. I couldn't understand why he held Michael Owen back. It didn't make sense to me. Owen should have started against Romania. When I wasn't commentating, I was screaming like every other England fan: 'Get Owen on!' Finally, Hoddle made the obvious move and Owen scored. Had the precocious player appeared for the full ninety minutes, I doubt England would have lost that match. That way, they would have avoided Argentina. Hoddle, being Hoddle, never properly acknowledged that he'd got it wrong.

The notion developed that England might have won the World Cup if Owen had been brought in sooner, or if Beckham hadn't been sent off, or if Campbell's goal hadn't been ruled out. It was nonsense. England might well have beaten Argentina, but would they have beaten Holland? Or Brazil? Or France? To win the World Cup they would have needed to beat all three. In our dreams.

Yet Hoddle returned home something of a hero, and while those early results in the European Championship were poor, there was nothing that couldn't be rectified. As Kevin Keegan proved, however fortunately. Make no mistake, Hoddle committed professional suicide with his scandalous remarks in *The Times*: 'them things' which he 'never said' or didn't mean. But he had to go then. It would have been far better to have kept his ideas to himself.

Kevin Keegan seemed a natural choice as England manager. A player who'd achieved far more than his ability suggested that he could. So, he was clearly an inspirational, honest character and patriotic as anyone can be, but the question remains whether he is good enough as a coach.

You couldn't help but love watching Newcastle when Keegan was in charge. They were full of flair and adventure, exuding the belief that no matter how many goals the opposition scored Newcastle would score more. It was wonderful to see and all bar Manchester United fans wished that Newcastle would win the Premiership title. They didn't, blowing a twelve-point lead, and Keegan blew his top in a famous televised outburst at Elland Road during the run-in. I knew that night that they'd lost the title. It was such a pity.

What makes us believe that Keegan will be any different leading England?

CHAPTER TWENTY

IN THE LOW COUNTRIES WITH KEEGAN

During season 1999–2000, I had to fend off more than the occasional accusation that I suddenly had a downer on the game and was doing more than my usual share of moaning. The respect I held for some of my accusers made me stop and think. But no, I knew I could look into the mirror to ask myself the question and *still* say no. I say this fairly often but I wonder if anyone really listens. I don't go to games with general pre-conceived notions, I merely react to what I see. So, if in the last year or so I've been heard to moan more often, I promise it's because I've been watching more than my fair share of indifferent matches.

However, I will admit that I approached Euro 2000 in a slightly less than enthusiastic manner. There were many reasons. I'd been working very hard in my commentaries, on my Friday evening programme and the various writing commitments, as well as helping set up a new website. What I needed was a break, a holiday, not a highly intensive football tournament.

Further, as I get older, I actually find it more difficult leaving my family behind. With a European Championship or a World Cup, you can kiss goodbye to them for a month or more. Though my kids are probably accustomed to my being absent (and probably chuffed at the prospect!), it's getting harder for me. Much though I love the game, and enjoy the lifestyle that accompanies my involvement in it, I long for the days when I don't have to say: 'I'll see you soon.' I'm in tears as they head for another day at school.

Less important personally, I was uneasy too about England's prospects and the atmosphere they'd be playing in. The rioting in Istanbul and in Copenhagen didn't augur well for an event that threatened to drown in football violence. Sadly, England supporters have too often been the focus for that trouble, whatever the extent of their guilt, and the England team shoulders that baggage wherever they play.

In the circumstances, I didn't like the somewhat gung-ho approach of Kevin Keegan who, at times, acts more like a cheerleader than a coach. Of course, he despises the hooligans as much as anyone else and, just before the England party set off for their base at Spa in Belgium, he rightly went out of his way to pillory them. But Keegan, metaphorically, wraps himself up in the Union Flag like the best of them. He exudes patriotism and tends to deride those who don't wear the colours quite as fervently. Realism hardly ever infects his vocabulary. It didn't seem to matter that England had played so abysmally in the qualifying tournament, or had unconvincingly scrapped past Scotland in the play-offs. Only one of the sixteen managers that I heard predicted that his team would win the Championship – Keegan. He thought there wasn't too much to fear.

And I suspect, whatever he said publicly, he hated those of us, me included, who queried Alan Shearer's continued presence in the starting line-up. The coach will have seen such dissent as, at best, unhelpful so close to a major tournament, at worst, unpatriotic – even anti-English. He may not have appreciated that it was our dearest wish to have the captain ram that criticism straight back down our throats. That would mean both he and England would be doing well. To be honest, I never envy Mike Ingham his daily round of England press conferences during a World Cup or a European Championship. While the football correspondent must search his substantial intellect to find further fresh questions to ask, I'm off watching the other teams. So, I'd already seen both co-hosts in action, Belgium and Holland, before joining Mike in Eindhoven for his first game, England against Portugal.

Keegan's tactical awareness has been under question since he first took the England job – indeed, from long before. It must have been difficult blowing a twelve-point lead at the top of the Premiership while manager of Newcastle United. Akin, I suppose, to being two goals up within eighteen minutes against Portugal and losing 3–2. Keegan's two immediate predecessors as national coach, Terry Venables and Glenn Hoddle, happened to be staying at the same hotel in Amsterdam as I was. While I may have held reservations about both, I'm certain neither of them would have allowed their England teams to lose a game after going two-up.

Yet, before the match, there were optimistic noises emerging from the camp. The whispered word was that, while England would ostensibly line up 4-4-2, they would seamlessly switch to the more flexible 3-5-2 once they were in possession. Was this a sign that Keegan knew more than some of us thought? Did that stubborn exterior disguise a more pragmatic approach? I searched in vain for confirmation during the ninety minutes. If England changed tactics, the alteration was so subtle that nobody noticed. Instead, what we witnessed was a midfield outplayed and over-run, and a defence that creaked so badly you sensed Eindhoven must be situated above one of the planet's fault zones. England didn't merely lose 3–2; they were thrashed. Once again, all that flag-waving optimism was dismissed for what it represented: words without substance. I yearned for the nous of Venables or Hoddle.

I pitied Mike having to return to Spa amid the gloom. It was different for me and for our England summariser, Terry Butcher. No one waves the flag as much as this particular former England captain but, away from the something atmosphere of the England camp, we could still retain our objectivity. The Portugal match had been wonderful to watch. We oozed with admiration for Figo and Rui Costa and regretted, with the admirable exception of David Beckham, that England hadn't a player to rival their quality. Finishing a wretched nine points behind Sweden in the qualifying group wasn't misleading. England really were that bad.

Now, at the start of a European Championship that, in football terms, had the makings of being the best ever seen, England's shortcomings had been radically exposed. They'd be up against the delights of the world champions, France, who'd won in 1998 without having a striker worthy of the name. Now they had Thierry Henry and Nicolas Anelka. The French were frightening in the demolition of former champions Denmark. And there was Holland. Certainly, they were fortunate to beat the Czechs in their opening game but, man for man, better than England in almost every position. My other favourites were Spain yet, being Spain, they initially succumbed to the tediously dull but effectively organised Norwegians. Which would we rather have? An England that bores you to death but wins 1–0 or a side that is frighteningly open and loses 3–2? Wasn't there a compromise?

After the defeat by Portugal, the German game had even more

riding on it. Indeed, you might say that it already had too much. I was in Rotterdam the night before for the meeting of Holland and Denmark. Though the De Kuip Stadium had altered radically from the time I watched England play there under Graham Taylor, I remembered vividly the tensions of that evening; England fans in town and hooliganism on the menu. What a contrast in Euro 2000. Though you could tell there was reasonably strict segregation, four-fifths of the ground a mass of bright orange and the rest in red, pockets of Dutch and Danish supporters found themselves sitting in the wrong areas. Had some of our notorious fans been in that position, you'd have guaranteed there'd be trouble. The Dutch and the Danes? Not a chance. No, this was the 'celebration of football' that UEFA had intended. Both national anthems were accorded complete respect and there wasn't a hint of misbehaviour during the match. All I was worried about was how the stadium literally moved when the fans danced and sang. The Feyenoord Stadium vibrates!

Then, shortly after full-time, news filtered through that there was fighting on the streets of Brussels and Charleroi. Sadly, it came as no surprise. Any fool would have seen it coming. Travelling abroad with England, all decent people, journalists as well as supporters, almost have their apologies rehearsed in advance. If trouble doesn't kick off, then *that* is the surprise.

I switched the television on as soon as I returned to my hotel in Amsterdam and sat through the news reports feeling thoroughly depressed. It was as if, in a personal sense, I was anticipating the official UEFA response made a couple of nights later. I was shouting: 'Enough!' Yes, there have been many worse occasions of violence. Marseille was only two years ago and Copenhagen two months before, but my patience had worn out. So, we were to learn, had UEFA's.

One scene sticks in my mind. It was of two men walking down the middle of a Brussels thoroughfare, chests thrust forward, shoulders pinned back. They may as well have been carrying a banner – 'We are Ingerland (sic). Who wants some?' I was ashamed and I was angry. How dare these people besmirch the sport they purport to follow and the nation they claim to love and represent. I am sick to death of these thugs. They ruin everything for genuine supporters who are stained by association. They make lives a misery for the citizens of the towns and cities through which they rampage. By what right are they allowed to carry on?

As I've said earlier, I have voted Labour all my life. However, in relation to the way I'd treat these people, I'm to the right of Attila the Hun. Never mind their civil liberties, what about the liberties of everyone else? Take away their passports. Better still, burn their passports! If the law needs changing, then change it. Hooliganism is a disease, the 'English disease' as it is so embarrassingly referred to. Untreated, it will kill football.

So, it was with more dread than usual that we made our way to Charleroi. It proved, as so many anticipated, a ridiculous venue for so high-profile a fixture. Yet, on what grounds were we complaining? In a football sense? It's true that, in terms of quality, the stadium would have ranked far down the list of, say, the first division. But that's not why we feared Charleroi. We could tell that the narrow streets of the town would provide an ideal battleground for those who wanted to fight, for those who had little or no intention of watching the football.

Even in the glow of a rare competitive win against Germany, the first for thirty-four years, I felt flat. Firstly because, unlike the meetings in 1970, 1990 and 1996, nothing was decided by England's victory. They'd still need a point from the match with Romania in order to reach the last eight. Secondly, I was worried about what might be happening outside the stadium, around

Charleroi and, further away, in the Belgian capital.

Somehow, we got lost in Brussels on the way back to our hotel. We stopped the car to ask a policeman, a riot policeman. It was surreal. As he glanced at our map and pointed to the way 'home', sirens were blaring, dogs were barking, blue lights flashing and a water cannon was being moved into position. It's no wonder UEFA's executive committee was provoked into agreeing to hold an emergency meeting and they drew the logical conclusion: they issued a barely disguised threat to kick England out of the tournament should there be any further serious trouble.

If England fans cannot behave when they are abroad (and I'm not talking about the thousands of innocent supporters who sat in that Charleroi Stadium offering the team fantastic support), if the UK government doesn't take sufficient action to stop these troublemakers travelling, then the authorities are right to question whether the English team should be allowed to compete. Like them, I too am exasperated.

This was a time when Keegan could have helped, not by beating the drum and trumpeting his belief that England could now win the European Championship, but by dampening expectations. And with good reason. England didn't play that well against Germany. They didn't have to. The Germans were awful, wretchedly failing to turn 61% of the possession into a single goal. Unquestionably, it was the worst German team we've seen for many generations. Keegan should have been saying: 'Look, don't get carried away. It's wonderful to beat Germany, but we had a fair bit of luck. About time too! But let's not underestimate the Romanians. I've always thought, deep down, that we do have a chance of winning this thing, but there's a very long way to go.' Unfortunately, that's not Kevin's style.

England fell to earth with a nasty bump against Romania. Once more they failed to hold on to a lead. Once more their resources and 'tactics' proved woefully inadequate. One of the most enduring images I took from Euro 2000 was the sight of Kevin Keegan standing by the touchline, puffing out his chest and pointing to his heart – 'More effort lads! Do it for England!' As if such a gesture could stop the tidal wave of Portuguese and Romanian attacks.

Only once during England's games, for a brief time against Germany, did England alter their formation to make you think Keegan just might know what he was doing. He replaced Owen (though it should have been Shearer) with Gerrard and pushed Scholes a little further forward into the old Sheringham role. At least, numerically, the team was now able to compete in the vital midfield area. Unfortunately, Scholes picked up a slight injury and England reverted to Keegan's favoured 4-4-2. Anyone could see that in all three matches England needed five players across the middle, whether by 4-5-1 or 3-5-2, but Keegan didn't.

There've been times when I've felt hurt and disappointment as England made their exit from a major tournament, as in 1990 and 1996, when the breaks and the penalty shoot-outs didn't go their way, when they deserved better. Not this time. Instead, I felt flat and resigned to the fate of a team badly directed and patently not good enough. How could Euro 2000 miss an outfit so embarrassingly out of its depth?

Amazingly, at his final press conference, Keegan had the nerve to suggest that England had 'developed under me'. But I'm sure I'm not the only one to think they've regressed by about six years. The England team that departed the Low Countries was in as bad a state as it's been in since 1994 and they will have entered the qualifying campaign for the next World Cup with dubious hopes of reaching South Korea and Japan.

Of course, as you'd expect, the Football Association stands by its man, probably because they can't think of anyone else to turn to.

Sadly, in particular, they're clearly determined not to turn back to Venables, a far better man for the job. However, one of the chief lessons to be learnt from the Euro 2000 experience was that Keegan needs to have more than just 'ra-ra' if he's to have the remotest chance of succeeding. The players he has available, with their limited ability and technique, still can and should do better. If the coach has little tactical acumen, then get someone in alongside him who does, like Don Howe or someone similar.

Clearly, there isn't much further to fall so, logically, the only way is up. I doubt Keegan will make radical changes in personnel, even though he should. As well as Shearer, and for varying reasons of age, fitness and injury, Adams, Ince, Keown and Seaman should also be consigned to the international dustbin. Let's get players like Gareth Barry and Steven Gerrard into the team quickly. And when, please, will an England coach learn how to employ the talents of Rio Ferdinand?

It's sad but true that UEFA and Belgium breathed a huge sigh of relief the minute England left for home. It meant they'd take their 'baggage' with them. After the Romania game in Charleroi, the local mayor announced that he had found the England fans 'charming' and that they'd be welcome back anytime. He must have a very short memory span and it didn't stop him making advance and quite contradictory plans. As soon as he heard that the Mayor of Brussels had cancelled all trains between the two cities (an attempt to prevent England fans returning to the capital), the Mayor of Charleroi kindly laid on buses to remove supporters after the match free of charge – 'Nice to see you, now good riddance!'

I suspect that FIFA had already long made up its mind that England would not be staging the 2006 World Cup, but the behaviour of those fans in Belgium emphasised one of the two reasons why I believe the Football Association's bid campaign was fatally flawed and therefore certain to fail. Publicly or otherwise, what we were really saying was this: 'Bring the World Cup to us where we can control the hooligans. Stage it anywhere else and we can't be held responsible.' It was a morally indefensible position.

Almost as bad, and however much the FA maintained that it never happened, the former chairman Sir Bert Millichip did promise that if Germany supported England for Euro 96 we would back them for the World Cup ten years later. The Germans kept their promise; we didn't. How could FIFA and UEFA fail to notice? We didn't deserve to get the World Cup.

Meanwhile, back in the Low Countries, and with that FIFA announcement still weeks away, I was in need of a substantial tonic and it came quickly, the following evening in Bruges. Ever since, I've been searching my brain trying to think if I've ever seen a better game of football and I've concluded that I haven't, or at least I don't remember it. Spain against Yugoslavia had everything.

The match was played at a furious pace as both teams attacked at every opportunity, but the speed of the spectacle never smothered the magnificent technique that was also on display. This was 4-4-2 played at its very best and certainly not as it's played by England. I was actually relieved that Keegan's team wasn't in the tournament anymore. They couldn't have lived in that company. At 3–2 to Yugoslavia, who'd taken the lead for the third time despite having had a player sent off for the third game in succession, I saw that Spanish heads were beginning to drop, ever so slightly, but still noticeably. Moving into stoppage time, I suggested in the commentary that Spain couldn't do a Manchester United and score twice, as they'd need to do to reach the quarter-finals. I was very pleased to scrape the egg from my face afterwards.

Mendieta equalised with a penalty. I looked at my watch. With stoppages within stoppage time, I estimated that we maybe had two minutes left to play. I so wanted both sides to qualify and I knew that Yugoslavia would go through even if they lost the match. I was almost on my feet now, despite the very cramped commentary position that hemmed you in for hours at a time. Clutching the microphone in my right hand, I used my left to urge Spain forward just as the coach Camacho and everyone on the Spanish bench were doing. One last attack, a header down and a wonderful winning volley from Alfonso. I was standing screaming in delight. I don't ever remember being as excited or as pleased at seeing a goal – not even when Ole Gunnar Solskjaer scored the European Cup winner for Manchester United in the Nou Camp in 1999.

I knew that if I saw nothing else in the European Championship, then I'd still feel very privileged to have witnessed that moment, that game. The adrenaline was still pumping furiously over six hours later sharing a beer with Terry Butcher. We'd dismissed our disappointment over England. They were out, so what?

The Spanish win in Bruges set them up for a quarter-final clash with France in the same city and they would have taken another enthralling game into extra time if Raul hadn't missed with the last-minute penalty. Spain went home. As with the Czechs, who were so unfortunate to be drawn against France and Holland in the group phase, I was sorry to see the exit of an outstanding team. Yet, unquestionably, the best had survived to reach the last four. It's rare that you reach this stage without having preferences as to whom you would like to see go further but, genuinely, I didn't mind. I suppose a majority wanted to watch a France/Holland final. I'd have been just as happy with Italy/Portugal.

Both semi-finals were dramatic. Perhaps they lacked the out-standing quality of some of the games that had gone before, but Mike Ingham and I have commentated on too many semi-finals to be surprised at that. Tension takes over; there is so much at stake. I felt very sorry for Portugal who had contributed so much that was so good about the tournament. However, their reaction to the awarding of a penalty kick to France in extra time was disgraceful. I was commentating and the angle we viewed the incident from made it impossible to tell whether or not Abel Xavier had handled the ball and whether or not it had been done deliberately. As he should be, the linesman was in a good position to judge. Within seconds, the television replays showed him to be entirely correct. That didn't stop the Portuguese from going berserk.

There were two things that I highlighted at the time. Firstly, Xavier must have known the justice of the award yet he protested as vehemently as any of his colleagues. That is to his shame and he will have to live with it for the rest of his career. How can he tell the truth now? Anyway, with UEFA imposing a nine-month international ban on the player, ruling him out of several important World Cup qualifying games, that gave him plenty of time to consider the errors of his way. Secondly, those on the Portuguese bench immediately gathered around a television monitor presumably intent on seeing evidence that the linesman was wrong. They saw precisely what I did. How could they continue to rant and rave? It was pathetic and diluted my admiration for their previous performances. France deserved to go through.

The next night in Amsterdam, everything seemed set up for Holland. They'd scored six against Yugoslavia and looked at the top of their form. The atmosphere was incredible, the arena ablaze with the colour of orange and vibrating with passion and noise. The Italians had Zambrotta sent off after thirty minutes. I looked across to Mike who was commentating at this stage. 'Penalties,' I whispered, 'penalty shoot-out.' We'd still an hour of normal time to go and thirty minutes of extra time that might have produced a golden goal, but I had no doubts whatsoever. Indeed, the longer the game went without a goal being scored, as Holland missed two penalties and hit the post, the more certain I became. And the more my admiration grew for the magnificence of the Italian display. Later, I heard people say how disappointed they were that Italy had gone through, that their 'negative' approach was threatening to ruin the tournament. I couldn't agree. Of course, it's wonderful to witness fast-flowing attacking play, but this game of ours is also about defending and no one is better at defending than the Italians. Even while commentating, I took to physically applauding the interventions of Nesta and Cannavaro. Oh that England had that pair available to them!

The point was emphasised at the Championship climax in Rotterdam where Italy started so positively against the favourites. Francesco Totti overshadowed Zinedine Zidane as the man of the match and the Azzurri came within seconds of winning but France equalised in stoppage time and, as against Portugal in the semi-final, took the title on a 'golden goal', a spectacular effort from David Trezeguet. It was a fantastic finish to a wonderful game in an exceptional tournament. I thought it better than the 1984 event when, on home soil, France won for the first time. Better even than the 1970 World Cup, which has always been considered the best football finals there has ever been. Mexico certainly rivalled Euro 2000 in terms of technique but, thirty years on, the pace of the game has taken football on to a higher plane. Euro 2000 is now 'the best ever', though, perhaps, only until 2002 when it's South Korea and Japan.

I remember sitting at Rotterdam airport at 6 a.m. the morning after the game, waiting for an early flight home, physically exhausted and mentally drained at the efforts made over the previous three and a half weeks. The other passengers sipping coffee in the lounge, trying like me to stay awake, were no doubt equally as tired. How many, though, had been as privileged as myself? Watching a stunning festival of football from the best seats and being paid handsomely for doing so. No one need tell me about enjoying the good life.

CHAPTER TWENTY-ONE

WHERE TO NOW?

Twenty years ago, I couldn't have dreamt of the work I'd be doing now or the lifestyle I'd be leading. Even a decade ago, in the immediate aftermath of the sad death of Peter Jones that, in retrospect, was such a pivotal moment in my broadcasting career, I doubt I had any firm idea of what lay ahead. With that experience behind me, it won't be a surprise for you to learn that I have only the foggiest notion of what I'm doing next.

It doesn't worry me. With few exceptions, most of what's happened to me in my working life has been beneficial and exciting. Seriously, I can't complain. So, why should the future concern me?

Going freelance in 1997 was a key decision. I'd worked on the BBC staff for over twenty years and loved most of that time. Yet I knew, and the BBC knew, that I needed to kick in to another gear. It wasn't that I was stagnating but what I was doing had become too comfortable. Fresh stimulus was required. Financial and otherwise.

I was earning good money but, at that time, the BBC was structured in a manner that didn't always relate ability and experience to salary. Apart from annual across-the-board increments in line with inflation, and the occasional bonus, I had been stuck at the roof of my grade since 1982. In terms of my salary, there was actually nowhere else to go. It didn't matter if the Corporation wanted to pay me more, which they did, the pay structure wouldn't allow it.

Worse, as my profile rose, frequently I was being asked to do work outside the BBC. Slowly, I was building a freelance portfolio alongside my BBC staff existence: writing a column for newspapers or magazines, making public appearances, giving after-dinner speeches, whatever. Mostly, the BBC was happy for this to happen. It augmented my salary without them having to contribute and, crucially, it didn't conflict with my regular duties. But it became messy. I would have to submit copy to my head of department for editorial approval before it went to the magazine or newspaper that was actually paying me. There was a strict taboo on doing advertising voiceovers, a highly lucrative avenue that I found temporarily cut off. The BBC wasn't trying to be unfair, indeed far from it. I was being allowed to do lots of things that were ordinarily frowned upon. However, on those occasions when it had to say no – and I always sought BBC approval for what I was doing – increasingly large sums of money were at stake. Having to turn them down wasn't fair to me or to my family.

Together, the BBC and I decided to rationalise the situation. I would resign from the staff, take a contract to provide commentaries for them, and release myself to do anything else I fancied. It's worked really well and, I hope, on both sides. The BBC still employs me but it buys my services from my company. I am now free to write whenever and for whomever I like. Not, mind you, 'whatever'. I'm still guided by the boundaries of common sense and the need not to embarrass the BBC. I can now do voiceovers for ads, videos, computer games, CD-Roms. I can write a book like this without asking for permission. Being totally freelance has added incredible variety to what I do. I'm also far better paid.

★　★　★

But perhaps the most exciting development has arisen in the last year. I have never really considered myself to be computer literate. Watching my kids at the keyboard has been a truly humbling experience. When something goes wrong, I have a tendency to scream and shout, finally to collapse in a heap, distraught at my technological incompetence. Simon comes in, taps a key and all is well. For most of the time, I knew how to switch on my desktop PC and my laptop but only to use as glorified word processors, typewriters. No longer.

I had made occasional contributions to the BBC's website. It seemed no different from writing a newspaper column. I didn't really understand the 'Net' or the concept of 'hits'. It was something for the future, for my kids, for my retirement. Well, new technology doesn't hang around for long, it quickly becomes commonplace.

Within a couple of weeks, I received three quite separate approaches to be involved in new website ventures. I did as any freelance does – you immediately declare animated interest even if you expect that nothing of substance will happen. I was wrong. One of the companies quickly offered a contract that, for little work, almost matched the money I'd been making during the last year of my staff existence in the BBC. Now I had to pay attention.

A few days later, while turning this offer over in my mind, I presented Friday evening's *5 Live Sport*. Harry Harris, the chief football writer on the *Mirror*, and a long-time good friend of mine, was a guest on the programme. After the on-air conversation ended, and we'd gone to the regular Nationwide commentary, I asked Harry if he knew anything about the Internet. 'Funny you should mention that . . .'

Harry was already deep into thinking about the Net and we quickly discovered that we thought along similar lines. The complications of the technology were for others to deal with. We simply had a basic core idea. Football is about opinions. Some, usually ventured on interminable radio phone-ins hosted by ego-tripping presenters, are hardly worth hearing. What was needed, we thought, was a means of getting substantial and sensible football opinion on-line. The result is *www.voiceoffootball.com*.

The site went on-line in May 2000. It's centred on a small group of like-minded people. Some are, definitively, computer literate. Others are hardheaded businessmen. A couple, like Harry and me, are mere journalists. What we all share in common is a passion for football and for talking about football. In terms of money, we've invested next to nothing: major companies like Umbro, Carling, Nationwide and Gillette were rushing to come on board once they heard our ideas. In terms of effort? Well, how much effort is involved when you're having fun? That for me, and for Harry, is the key. We started VOF because we thought it would be a fun, stimulating thing to do. We were genuinely amazed when we found out you might actually make good money as well.

If I believe even some of what our business advisors tell us, we can all think of early retirement. But, honestly, that would be anathema to me. I hope to be commentating until I drop down dead. Everything I've achieved has been due to my love of football and my good fortune in being able to express that love in a certain manner. It's one of the reasons I take such offence at those who think I only ever moan about the game. They're not really listening to what I'm saying. They certainly don't know Alan Green. Hopefully, you do a little better now.

INDEX